THE QUIZ OF ENCHANTMENT

PUBLISHED BY

NEW MEXICO MAGAZINE

D1042676

ThE QUIZ OF ENChAntmENt

BY MICHAEL McDONALD

**EDITED BY
ARNOLD VIGIL**

**PRODUCED AND ILLUSTRATED BY
RICHARD C. SANDOVAL**

**PHOTOGRAPHY BY
MARK NOHL**

**TYPESETTING BY
LINDA J. VIGIL**

C O N T E N T S

First paperback edition 1992
by *New Mexico Magazine*

Copyright © by *New Mexico Magazine*
New Mexico Magazine

ISBN 0-937206-23-7

Library of Congress Catalog
Card Number 91-067865

New Mexico Magazine
1100 St. Francis Drive
Santa Fe, New Mexico 87503

PREFACE

By Marc Simmons

"I think New Mexico was the greatest experience from the outside world that I have ever had. It certainly changed me forever," wrote English novelist D.H. Lawrence. Many people today, natives and visitors alike, probably can claim they know exactly what he was talking about because they've had their own deep-felt love affair with New Mexico. The state is such a very special place that writers, artists, scholars and just about everyone else with a few grains of sensitivity can't help being profoundly touched by it.

Getting to know New Mexico's many faces offers the pleasure of exploration and discovery. Landscape and natural wonders, history, native cultures, art and a regional architecture are just some of the lures that can quickly engage one's interest. As we move about, looking and learning, our knowledge deepens and as it does our appreciation seems to grow for what New Mexico was and is, and represents.

Michael McDonald of Santa Fe is one of those who has met the state on its own terms and continues to benefit from his encounter. As part of his explorations, he began compiling several years ago a collection of New Mexican trivia—key questions, brainteasers really—that allow a testing of one's knowledge in a variety of areas. He would be the first to admit that there is nothing solemn or weighty in all of this, for in fact a trivia question is meant to entertain and only secondarily to inform.

But inform, these little nuggets of trivia do. They naturally arouse our curiosity and point us toward New Mexican pathways worth a closer and more serious examination. And besides, matching wits with McDonald is just plain fun. So, whether you are learning about New Mexico for the first time or you are an old hand, well-schooled in local lore, this handy and challenging little book is one to savor.

1
BEGINNINGS

New Mexico is one of the oldest places of habitation on the North American continent. This section will tell you of its origins and of the beginnings of other institutions in the state.

Q: What famous ancient Indian settlement is located north of Silver City?
A: The Gila Cliff Dwellings.

Q: Where were the first horses introduced into Western America and first used by the Indians?
A: Along the Río Grande.

Q: What is considered the oldest continually occupied dwelling in America?
A: Ácoma Pueblo.

Q: Who traveled through New Mexico in search of the fabled Seven Cities of Cíbola?
A: Francisco Vázquez de Coronado.

Q: What turned out to be only a "huddle of mud huts" during Coronado's expedition?
A: The Seven Gold Cities of Cíbola.

Q: Who was the Spaniard who led the colonization of New Mexico?
A: Juan de Oñate.

Q: What was San Juan de los Caballeros?
A: The first European settlement in New Mexico.

Q: In 1593, the name of this pueblo was Bové. What is it today?
A: San Ildefonso.

Q: Oñate gained the first right to what personal titles in New Mexico?
A: Governor and captain general.

Q: In the late 1630s, Gov. Luís de Rosas used Indian slave labor in what New Mexico city?
A: Santa Fe.

Q: Rosas also beat two friars with a stick until they were "bathed in blood." What happened to Rosas in 1641?
A: He was murdered.

Q: What famous New Mexico event occurred Aug. 10, 1680?
A: The Pueblo Revolt.

Q: How many Spaniards were killed during the revolt?
A: 400.

The Gila Cliff Dwellings National Monument north of Silver City once was home to the Mogollón Indians.

Q: What happened to the remainder of the Spanish?
A: They were driven out of the province to El Paso.

Q: Who is generally regarded as the Indian leader of the revolt?
A: Popé of San Juan.

Q: What was the primary motive for the Indians' rebellion?
A: Religious freedom.

Q: What nomadic tribe joined the Pueblos against the Spanish?
A: Apache.

Q: How many years did the Indians hold out?
A: Thirteen.

Q: In 1693, Santa Fe was retaken from the Indians under the leadership of what newly appointed governor?
A: Diego de Vargas.

Q: What well-known religious statue was returned to Santa Fe by Vargas?

A: La Conquistadora (Our Lady of the Conquest).

Q: Although Vargas' reconquest has been called "bloodless," how many Indians were killed?
A: Eleven were killed during the actual battle, but 70 were executed by order of Vargas afterwards.

Q: Where did the battle take place?
A: At the walled city of Santa Fe.

Q: What happened to the 400 Indian survivors after the Battle for Santa Fe?
A: They were made slaves for 10 years.

Q: In 1780-1781, the worst epidemic on record in New Mexico took the lives of thousands of Spanish settlers and Pueblo Indians. What was the disease?
A: Smallpox.

Q: Dr. Cristóval Larrañaga brought the new smallpox vaccine to New Mexico from Chihuahua City in 1804. Due to the lack of refrigera-

The arrival of conquistadores and other European explorers forever changed the fate of the state's Native Americans.

tion to preserve the vaccine, how did he transport it?

A: By vaccinating small children and taking them on the journey.

Q: In the 1780s, King Charles III of Spain made an unusual request of New Mexico Gov. Juan Bautista de Anza to send him something. What was it?

A: Eight elk for his zoo in Madrid.

Q: Who was the founder of the Gurulé family name in New Mexico?

A: The Frenchman Jacques Grolé (or Grolet) who married Elena Gallegos in the late 1600s.

Q: What group of New Mexican hunters wore painted leather hats with feathers, similar to what Robin Hood wore?

A: *Los Ciboleros* (buffalo hunters).

Q: With what weapon did *Los Ciboleros* kill buffalo?

A: The lance.

Q: When was Albuquerque established?

A: In 1706.

Q: Who was the Viceroy of New Spain (Mexico) in 1706?

A: The Duke of Alburquerque.

Q: Coronado came to New Mexico in search of the Seven Cities of Cíbola. What is the best translation of the name Cíbola?

A: Buffalo.

Q: What is the name of an early culture in New Mexico that dates back 25,000 years?

A: Sandía Man.

Q: Sandía Man's artifacts were found at Sandía Cave. Where is Sandía Cave?

A: Between Placitas and Sandía Peak.

Q: What was the third European settlement in the United States?

A: Taos.

Q: Who was the first U.S. Catholic priest in New Mexico in 1851?

A: Jean Baptiste Lamy.

Q: In 1860, Archbishop Lamy planned and helped build what famous building in Santa Fe?

A: St. Francis Cathedral.

Q: What religious order brought Catholicism to New Mexico?
A: The Franciscans.

Q: Why did tourism gain in popularity after 1879?
A: The arrival of the railroad in the state.

Q: Capt. Gaspar Pérez de Villagrá wrote the first historical account of New Mexico in what year?
A: He penned an epic poem named *Historia* in 1610.

Q: The remains of an ancient people believed to have existed 15,000 years ago were discovered in 1926 near Folsom, N.M. What do anthropologists call this ancient race of hunters?
A: Folsom Man.

Q: What is the Folsom point?
A: The distinct "flint dart" point used by Folsom Man.

Q: Who actually discovered the Folsom Man site and in what year?
A: A black cowboy who went by the name George McJunkin, in 1908.

George McJunkin is credited with discovering the site of Folsom Man, where humans lived about 15,000 years ago.

B. HUGHES

Q: Folsom Man might have been called Ragtown Man had the discovery been made earlier. Why?

A: Ragtown was Folsom's former name.

Q: What could have been considered unusual (at that time in history) about George McJunkin?

A: He was treated as an equal among his cowboy peers and was an intellectual. He carried a telescope on his saddle, played the violin and was well-read.

Q: The year 1598 was important to Old San Juan north of Española. Why?

A: It was when Spain established the first capital of New Mexico. (Santa Fe was not the first capital.)

Q: How old is the still-occupied Taos Pueblo?

A: More than 800 years old.

Q: Padre Antonio José Martínez was a prominent Taoseño who created two firsts for Taos. What are they?

A: He started the first co-educational school west of the Mississippi and he printed the Southwest's first newspaper *El Crepusculo de Libertad.*

Q: Old Town in Albuquerque was built around the San Felipe de Neri Church on the banks of the Rio Grande. What caused modern downtown to develop farther east?

A: Railroad officials decided the land near the river was too soft to lay rails on so they installed tracks farther east.

Q: In what unusual fashion were the first telephone lines of Lordsburg strung?

A: They were draped along existing barbed-wire fences.

Q: The Spanish began building Santa Fe how many years before the Pilgrims established Plymouth Rock?

A: Ten. Santa Fe was founded in 1610.

BUILDING A STATE

It took many years of struggle to make New Mexico a state. It was first the land of the Indians, then a Spanish colony, then a Mexican territory, then a U.S. territory and finally the 47th state. During its fight to become a state it experienced 60 years as a territory of the United States. Many interesting events occurred during that time. These are just some of them.

Q: Who led the first Anglo-American expedition into New Mexio in 1806?
A: Zebulon Pike.

Q: Who did President James K. Polk put in command of the Army of the West?
A: Col. Stephen Watts Kearny.

Q: In what New Mexico town did Kearny make public the United States' intention to make New Mexico a U.S. territory?
A: Las Vegas.

Q: Who was the Mexican governor of New Mexico at the time the United States took possession?
A: Manuel Armijo.

Q: What historic event occurred in Santa Fe on Aug. 18, 1846?
A: The U.S. flag was first raised over the capital city, declaring the conquest of New Mexico complete.

Q: Who was the first appointed governor of the new territory?
A: Charles Bent.

Q: What happened to Gov. Bent in Taos five months later?
A: He was murdered and scalped during a rebellion against the United States.

Q: Who murdered Gov. Bent?
A: Taos Pueblo Indians under the leadership of Tomasito.

Q: Who described New Mexico in 1862 as "a country which is not worth the life of one good man"?
A: A Confederate officer under Gen. Henry Sibley's command after the Confederacy lost the New Mexico campaign during the Civil War.

Q: What year did Padre Martínez first declare New Mexico for statehood?
A: 1849.

Q: In a spirit of Anglo-Saxon superiority, New Mexico was criticized as the home of illiterate "half-breeds, greasers, outlaws" who comprised "the tag end of all that is objectionable in an imperfect civilization." What caused these outbursts?
A: New Mexico's quest for statehood.

Q: What place-name came from the Aztec words meaning "place of the

The Taos Plaza remains the center of activity.

moon" or "center of the moon"?

A: Mexico.

Q: What river was the boundary line between Mexico and the United States after the Cessions of 1848?

A: The Gila.

Q: New Mexico Territory of 1850-1861 included parts of Colorado and Nevada and what other entire state?

A: Arizona.

Q: What state laid claim to most of New Mexico due to the Treaty of Velasco in 1836?

A: Texas.

Q: In 1857, a proposed division of the New Mexico Territory would have left the Grand Canyon in New Mexico and put Carlsbad Caverns and White Sands in what territory?

A: Arizona.

Q: In 1852, five of the nine counties of New Mexico were somewhat

New Mexico, Lincoln, Jefferson and Montezuma were among the names considered during the quest for statehood.

unusual: Taos, Bernalillo, Valencia, Socorro and Doña Ana. Why?
A: They covered the entire width of the territory from east to west.

Q: In 1873, New Mexico Territorial delegate Stephen Elkins was sent to Washington to rally voters for a certain bill. At one point he publicly congratulated a Northern congressman for a fiery speech he had given that viciously attacked the South. Later, a Southern congressman voted against it, and thereby caused defeat for, the bill Elkins favored. What extremely important bill did Elkins political blunder kill?
A: Statehood for New Mexico.

Q: What names were seriously considered, other than New Mexico, when proposals for statehood were made?
A: Lincoln, Jefferson and Montezuma.

Q: In 1875, companies L and M of the 8th Cavalry were stationed at Fort Union. Under what department at that time did all military forces in New Mexico operate?
A: The Department of Missouri.

Col. Teddy N. Roosevelt, center, in front of the Castañeda Hotel in Las Vegas, N.M., at the first Rough Riders Reunion in June 1899. (Museum of New Mexico photo, Neg. No. 14292.)

Q: During the Spanish-American War, a certain elite fighting corps was chosen out of a group of volunteers from Arizona, New Mexico and Oklahoma. What were they called?
A: The Rough Riders.

Q: Who led the Rough Riders?
A: Theodore Roosevelt.

Q: In 1899, the Rough Riders held a reunion in what New Mexico town?
A: Las Vegas.

Q: During the Rough Riders Reunion, what did Theodore Roosevelt promise the people of New Mexico?
A: To help them gain statehood.

Q: Did he succeed?
A: No.

Q: What did the Jointure Act of 1905 propose?
A: That New Mexico and Arizona become one large state.

U.S. Army Gen. William Tecumseh Sherman tried to persuade military leaders to give New Mexico back to Mexico in 1864.

Q: What defeated this effort for statehood?
A: The people of Arizona overwhelmingly rejected it.

Q: What was one of the main arguments against statehood?
A: It would raise taxes.

Q: In 1864, what did Gen. William Tecumseh Sherman recommend to the House Military Affairs Committee in regards to New Mexico?
A: To prevail upon Mexico to take it back.

Q: What did writer Edith M. Nicholl observe about New Mexico in 1898?
A: That it was "unsupported by intelligence" and was a "most solitary waste."

Q: What was New Mexico, according to an 1871 *New York Times* editorial?
A: The "heart of our worst civilization."

Q: Who wrote, "Curious as it may sound, it was New Mexico that liberated me from the present era of civilization"?

Writer D.H. Lawrence and his wife Frieda.
(Photograph courtesy of the Witter Bynner Foundation.)

A: D.H. Lawrence.

Q: In 1869, Colfax County was created and named for Schuyler Colfax. Who was Schuyler Colfax?
A: Vice president of the United States.

Q: In 1882, a territorial delegate election caused quite a stir in the village of Rito Quemado where 30 voters lived. What was the controversy?
A: A total of 257 votes was cast for one of the candidates.

Q: By a vote of more than 2-to-1, what did the citizens of New Mexico approve on Jan. 21, 1911?
A: The state constitution.

Q: What happened at the White House at 1:35 p.m. Jan. 6, 1912?
A: President William Howard Taft signed the proclamation making New Mexico the 47th state.

Q: Who was New Mexico's first state governor?
A: William C. McDonald of Lincoln County.

Q: Octaviano Larrazolo, New Mexico's fourth governor, holds a distinction among his fellow governors. What is it?
A: The only foreign-born governor (in Mexico 1859).

Q: What new form of communications was introduced in Santa Fe in 1881?
A: The telephone.

Q: During the 1890s, what New Mexico city became the first to use electric lights?
A: Albuquerque.

Q: Thomas B. Catron and Albert B. Fall became the first to hold what office when New Mexico became a state?
A: U.S. senator.

Q: The motto *Crescit Eundo* is on the Great Seal of the State of New Mexico. What does it mean?
A: We grow as we go.

Q: What is the symbol on the state flag called?

Roots of the yucca plant have kept people's hair clean in New Mexico for centuries.

A: Zía (a Pueblo sun symbol representing perfect friendship).

Q: The colors of the state flag are red and yellow. What origin does this have?
A: They were the colors of Queen Isabella of Castile and were carried by the first Spaniards to enter New Mexico.

Q: The state song is "O Fair New Mexico." Who wrote it?
A: Miss Elizabeth Garrett, the blind daughter of Sheriff Pat Garrett.

Q: The state flower is the yucca. The roots of this plant have been used for centuries as what?
A: Soap.

Q: The piñon (*Pinus edulis*) is the state tree. It burns with a wonderful fragrance, but what is its most tasteful product?
A: The piñon nut, which has been used as food for centuries.

Q: What well-known fowl is the state bird?
A: The roadrunner.

Q: The state fish is the *Salmo clarkii.* What's that?
A: The cutthroat trout.

Q: The state animal is the black bear. What famous black bear originated in New Mexico?
A: Smokey Bear.

Q: New Mexico has two state vegetables. What are they?
A: Chile and *frijoles* (beans).

Q: The state gem is well-known and closely associated with New Mexico. What is it?
A: Turquoise.

Q: What state organization celebrated its 50th anniversary in 1985 and its members still wear bow ties?
A: The New Mexico Department of Public Safety (state police).

Q: The sun symbol, which is the official symbol for the state, originated where?
A: At Zía Pueblo.

Q: What is the popular nickname for the state capitol?
A: The Roundhouse, because it is in the round shape of the ceremonial kiva.

The New Mexico State Capitol is also dubbed The Roundhouse because of its shape and similarity to a Pueblo kiva.

STATE FISH
Cutthroat Trout

STATE MAMMAL
Black Bear

STATE BIRD
Roadrunner

STATE FLOWER
Yucca

STATE VEGETABLE
Chile

STATE VEGETABLE
Pinto Bean

STATE INSECT
Tarantula Hawk Wasp

STATE FOSSIL
Coelophysis

STATE GEM
Turquoise

3

INDIANS

One of the most important cultures of New Mexico is the Indian culture. They were the first inhabitants of the area and their life changed significantly after the Europeans came. These questions will deal with their beginnings, their customs, their conflicts with the white men and the contributions they have made to the state.

Santiago "Jimmy" McKinn with Apache children after being captured by the tribe on the Mimbres River in 1885.
(Photo by C.S. Fly; Museum of New Mexico photo, Neg. No. 11649.)

Q: Who is rumored to have been the final chief of the last free Apaches?
A: Charlie McComas, a white man raised by the Indians.

Q: Chato, the Apache subchief, kidnapped the 6-year-old McComas after killing the boy's parents near what New Mexico town?
A: Silver City.

Q: Jimmy McKinn, another child captive of the Apaches, had a famous photograph taken of him while still among the Apaches by Camillus Fly, whose photo studio in Tombstone, Ariz., played an important part in the gunfight at the OK Corral. From what New Mexico town did little Jimmy come?
A: Silver City.

Q: One summer in 1885, a band of Apaches led by Gerónimo killed 16 people near Silver City. By what unusual means did the soldiers of Fort Bayard track the Indians?
A: By finding candies dropped by the Indians, some of which were those heart-shaped kind with love mottoes stamped on them.

Q: Between 1492 until the mid-1800s, what destroyed 90 percent of the Indian population, including those from New Mexico tribes?
A: European diseases.

Q: Kit Carson was ordered to force the Indians of the Navajo tribe to make the infamous "long walk." Where did they go?
A: Fort Sumner.

Q: Navajos today register historical time by the period before the "long walk," and the time after the march. When did this catastrophic event take place?
A: 1864.

Q: What ancient New Mexican pueblo ruins were once considered to have been inhabited by a people who were 15 feet tall due to some bones unearthed at its site?
A: Pecos.

Q: What did the Pueblo Indians call the early Spanish settlers, due to the ritual of baptism?
A: Wet Heads.

Q: In the early 1800s, New Mexicans would often raid Navajo villages and made money doing it. How?
A: They sold the Indians as slaves for 400 *pesos* each.

Q: The Navajos of western New Mexico loved to gamble, especially on horse races. What particularly valuable property did they sometimes put up for stakes and often lose?
A: Their wives.

Q: The residents of Ácoma Pueblo obtained their village bell by going to Zacatecas, Mexico, and purchasing it with what unusual payment?
A: They paid the Mexicans with 12 captured Apache children.

Q: In 1840, an unlikely hero, named Lucario Montoya, aged 17 and weighing 120 pounds, saved his village of Cebolleta from future attacks by the powerful Ute tribe by performing what feat?
A: In a prolonged duel using various weapons, he single-handedly killed a much more powerful Ute chief.

Q: What were the two most dominant nomadic Indian tribes of the 19th century in New Mexico?
A: Apache and Navajo.

Some Navajo men were known to gamble away their wives.

Q: Who was described in 1862 as "being about five feet eight inches in height, always dressed rather commonly, clean shaven face, light hair and light gray eyes, with a quiet manner of speaking, and a slouchy walker"?

A: Kit Carson.

Q: Of whom was it said, "[His] grave is no longer amid sequestered shades of Boggville on the Arkansas. The remains were removed in the fall of 1868 to Taos, New Mexico, [his] home"?

A: Kit Carson.

Q: One of the first major social cultures to emerge in what is now New Mexico is popularly believed named after the Navajo word for "ancient" or "old ones." What is it?

A: Anasazi. (Indian scholars today, however, say the Navajo word *anaa* means "war" or "enemy," while there is no word for *sazi*. They say Anasazi can be interpreted as "enemies of our ancestors.")

Q: The Anasazi are divided into two groups. What are they?

A: The Basketmakers and the Pueblo.

Early Pueblo Indians lived in caves carved from hillsides of volcanic ash at Bandelier National Monument.

Q: The Great Pueblo Period in which this culture reached its zenith, took place during what time in history?
A: A.D. 1100 to 1300.

Q: What is considered the probable cause of the demise of the Great Pueblo culture, which depended upon farming as a livelihood?
A: Almost a century of drought between 1215 and 1299.

Q: The nomadic Apache and Navajo tribes then occupied the lands abandoned by the Anasazi. Where is it believed they come from?
A: Northwest Canada.

Q: The Pueblo Indians re-established themselves mostly in what part of New Mexico?
A: The upper Rio Grande.

Q: Why was it relatively easy from a geological standpoint, for the Pueblo Indians, to build cave dwellings on the Pajarito Plateau?
A: The cliffs are formed of soft volcanic ash, or tuff.

Q: What major building technique brought the Indians out of the caves?
A: Masonry.

Q: About when did this type of building begin?
A: 1300s.

Q: What was the major source of fur for these cliff dwellers' winter clothing?
A: The rabbit.

Q: In 1861, Cochise led 400 warriors on an attack on Pinos Altos that nearly wiped out the community. What derogatory term did the Indians refer to the white men in the area during that time?
A: "Los Goddamnies," probably because of the frequent use of the term by the Anglo inhabitants.

Q: Why was Cimarron important to the Mohuache Utes and Jicarilla Apaches?
A: It was the location of an Indian agency and they went there for food and clothing.

Q: The Apaches of New Mexico concocted an unusual candy made from the sweet juice of the mescal plant and what other unlikely ingredient?
A: Horse meat.

Q: There is a small ski area in northern New Mexico called Sipapu. What does *sipapu* mean?
A: According to Navajo and Pueblo Indian religious beliefs, *sipapus* are the original points of creation on Earth.

Q: Why are the confluence of the Colorado and Little Colorado rivers in Arizona and Blue Lake in the Sangre de Cristo Mountains of northern New Mexico so important to the Indians of these areas?
A: They are believed to be actual *sipapus*.

Q: What are the round, below-ground ceremonial buildings of the Pueblo Indians called?
A: Kivas.

Q: What do kivas represent?
A: *Sipapus*.

Q: In the Indian religions of New Mexico, what are the "gods in human form" called?

A: Kachinas.

Q: The *Koshare* are also Indian gods. Why would non-Indians consider them unusual gods?
A: They are clowns.

Q: French trappers referred to it in their diaries as early as 1740. It was shipped all over the West. No fiesta was complete without it. It was originally known as *Aguardiente*. What was it?
A: Taos Lightning, the most famous liquor of the West.

Q: Who once lived in a house at Rayado south of Cimarron and helped Lucien Maxwell tend his cattle (the house was restored by the scouts at Philmont Scout Ranch in 1949, and is today a museum)?
A: Kit Carson.

Q: Several Pueblo governors have "badges of office" that are passed to succeeding governors. They have handles with the inscription: "A. Lincoln Prst. USA 1863." What are they?
A: They are canes which were given to the seven Pueblo governors who held a conference with President Lincoln in Washington, D.C., in 1863, to settle boundaries.

Q: Jémez Pueblo is famous for what tribal rite—also a popular sport—in which Jémez participants compete nationally?
A: Running.

Q: Ácoma Pueblo became involved in a controversy in December 1987 that included the participation of presidential candidate Jesse Jackson and his organization The Rainbow Coalition. It had to do with part of the Pueblo's sacred ground being turned into a national monument. What is this area called?
A: El Malpais.

Q: Why should you be wary of silver work stamped with "reservation-made"?
A: It comes from a place in Japan actually renamed Reservation.

Q: A certain type of Zuñi necklace made with flat, wheellike beads became extremely popular during the 1960s and '70s. What are they called?
A: Heishi.

Q: What New Mexico Indian tribe has earned a reputation for making superior drums?

A: Cochití.

Q: What tribe is noted for making fine wood flutes?
A: Taos.

Q: Ancient Indian rock paintings, found in many places in New Mexico, are called pictographs. New Mexico also boasts numerous examples of rock carvings. What are these called?
A: Petroglyphs.

Q: What well-known form of Navajo ceremonial art is only temporary and, in fact, is destroyed after its use as a curing power?
A: Sand painting.

Q: Are the permanent sand paintings that are available for sale authentic?
A: No. The designs are altered to prevent sacrilege.

Known originally as Aguardiente, *Taos Lightning became the most famous liquor of the Wild West.*

4

A SPANISH STATE

ew Mexico is probably the most Spanish state in today's America. Spanish influence can be seen and heard from one end of the state to the other and this entire book is filled with it, but this section deals with some of the particularly unique aspects of the Spanish culture that can be experienced only in New Mexico.

Q: By what method did New Mexican villagers regulate their daily activities?
A: The ringing of the church bell.

Q: What did the particular tolling of bells called *doblar las campanas* mean?
A: Someone had died.

Q: In 1770, over half the bells used in New Mexico were discovered to be cracked. Why?
A: The ringing of them during freezing weather.

Q: One of New Mexico's most illustrious citizens during the latter half of the 1800s was a college graduate, second-in-command of the 1st Regiment of the New Mexico Volunteers, an interpreter for Gen. Stephen W. Kearny, a territorial delegate to Congress, a member of the New Mexico Legislature for eight sessions and considered by many to be the "bravest man around." In 1904 he was murdered, the case unsolved. Who was he?
A: Col. José Francisco Chávez.

Q: *Los Hermanos de Sangre* is a religious brotherhood better known by what name?
A: The *Penitentes*.

Q: Where are the majority of *Penitente* sects to be found?
A: In the northern mountain villages of New Mexico.

Q: According to Anglo residents of the territorial days, what were "dobes"?
A: Adobe buildings.

Q: A kind of thick cookie that could last up to a year was a staple among New Mexicans and used in trade with the Comanches. Today, with the addition of sugar and anise, it has become a Christmas favorite. What is it called?
A: *Bizcochito*, the state cookie.

Q: A drink called *atole* once was described as "the coffee of the Mexicans," and is still available on many menus in New Mexico. What is it?
A: A thin, blue cornmeal mush mixed with milk.

Q: The Spanish gave the early settlers from the United States a name based on the language spoken by them. What is the name?
A: Anglos.

Wooden carretas del muerte *(carts of death) are an integral part of New Mexican folk art.*

Q: The famous Colonial church of San José de Gracia in Las Trampas contains an important item that the villagers have named Refugio. What is it?
A: The bell.

Q: In Las Trampas, a hooded, female, wooden figure with drawn bow and arrow is known as Doña Sebastiana. What does she represent?
A: Death.

Q: The well-known wall decoration made from a cross of sticks and wound and woven with colorful yarn is called what?
A: *Ojo de Dios* (God's eye).

Q: What well-known New Mexican bird is called *paisano* by Spanish-speaking natives?
A: The roadrunner.

Q: In Taos, what was known as *tío vivo*, Spanish for lively uncle?
A: An antique merry-go-round.

A farolito, *left, is a paper, candlelit lantern popular during New Mexican Christmas season.* Bultos *are wooden depictions of saints.*

Q: What is probably the most common place-name in New Mexico?
A: Arroyo Seco.

Q: What does it mean?
A: Dry gully.

Q: What are *farolitos*?
A: The paper bag lights that line streets and houses during Christmas, made of sand poured into a brown paper bag with a lighted candle stuck in it.

Q: Canjilon is a village where the descendants of what famous Spanish conquistador are reputed to still live?
A: Diego de Vargas.

Q: What today is still the most popular form of old Spanish sculpture?
A: *Bultos*, wooden depictions of saints.

Q: What unusual mobile sculpture has been called a form of present-day Hispanic metal smithing?

Española is known as the lowrider capital of the state.

A: Lowrider cars.

Q: What town in New Mexico is especially noted for its lowriders?
A: Española.

5

OUR TOWN

Just as elsewhere in this country, each town or city in New Mexico has its own uniqueness. This section will ask you things you might not know about Grants, Truth or Consequences, Deming, Clayton, Madrid, Las Vegas or even Albuquerque or Santa Fe.

*The ghost town of Shakespeare never really prospered as a
mining settlement.*

Q: What mineral brought Silver City its fame as a mining town?
A: Silver.

Q: What mineral made Silver City prosper?
A: Copper.

Q: What are Mogollón and Shakespeare?
A: Ghost towns.

Q: Where is Smokey Bear State Park and the site of his grave?
A: Capitán.

Q: What is Santa Rita noted for?
A: A large open-pit copper mine.

Q: What made Magdalena such a rip-roaring town in the late 1800s?
A: It was a railhead for cattle much like Dodge City was in Kansas.

Q: In what New Mexico town did Judge Roy Bean run a mercantile
store?
A: Pinos Altos.

Q: What do Nutt, Graham, Swastika, Steins, Bland, Brilliant and Dolores all have in common?
A: They are New Mexican ghost towns.

Q: What New Mexican town was once described as "the most substantially built of all territorial towns outside Santa Fe"?
A: Silver City.

Q: In the 1890s, what happened to Main Street in Silver City?
A: It was washed out by a flood and today is a creek.

Q: What was Los Alamos before it became famous as "The Birthplace of the Atomic Bomb"?
A: It was a boys' ranch.

Q: What did the ghost town of Twining become?
A: Taos Ski Valley.

Q: What is Hatch noted for?
A: Chile.

Q: In 1833, air pollution, noise pollution and sanitation were dealt with in one of the Southwest's earliest municipal codes. Antonio Barreiro wrote these ordinances for what city?
A: Santa Fe.

Q: What town was named after the Tewa Indian words for "red willow place" and "down at the village"?
A: Taos.

Q: What town was named by Van C. Smith for his father from Omaha, Neb.?
A: Roswell.

Q: What well-known gathering place of today was named after the Spanish word for a gathering place?
A: Glorieta (literally a bower or arbor).

Q: What city's name means "holy faith" in Spanish?
A: Santa Fe.

Q: What is Santa Fe's official name?
A: La Villa Real de la Santa Fe de San Francisco de Asis.

Q: What city was founded on an abandoned Tano Indian village?
A: Santa Fe.

The Silver City Museum reflects a bygone era.

Q: What is the best translation of the name Albuquerque?
A: White oak.

Q: It was named after the Duke of Alburquerque. Where was the original area known as Alburquerque in 1706?
A: In Portugal (the area now lies in Spain).

Q: What was the population of Albuquerque in 1706?
A: 252.

Q: What community at the foot of Old Baldy Peak, a.k.a. Sierra Blanca Mountain, means "noisy" in Spanish and is descriptive of the fast-flowing creek running through town?
A: Ruidoso.

Q: For whom or what was Gallup named?
A: David L. Gallup, paymaster for the A & P Railroad.

Q: What city was once a guarded secret and was closed to all public traffic?

The San Felipe de Neri Church once was the hub of Albuquerque.

A: Los Alamos.

Q: What does *los alamos* mean in English?
A: Poplars or cottonwoods.

Q: Wooden crosses were found over the graves of a Spanish caravan attacked by Indians. What city was established here?
A: Las Cruces.

Q: What city was originally known in English as "Our Lady of Sorrows of the Meadows"?
A: Las Vegas (the meadows).

Q: What city, founded in 1902, was at one time called Six-Shooter Siding?
A: Tucumcari.

Q: Truth or Consequences changed its name in the 1950s from Hot Springs because of the influence of what television emcee?

A: Ralph Edwards.

Q: To what New Mexico town was everybody going in John Ford's movie *Stagecoach*?
A: Lordsburg.

Q: What city named in 1598 means "help or aid" in Spanish?
A: Socorro.

Q: Albuquerque lies at the foot of Sandía Peak. What does *sandía* mean in English?
A: Watermelon.

Q: This town was the site of the famous gunbattle in which Elfego Baca held off a mob of Texas cowboys for 33 hours. What is its name?
A: Reserve.

Q: What town is named after the Spanish word for mouse?
A: Ratón.

Q: What village, once known as Levy, is the Spanish approximation of the Keresan Indian word for "place where there is water"?
A: Pecos.

Q: A group of New Mexican Sherlock Holmes enthusiasts often meet in what town?
A: Moriarty.

Q: There is a New Mexico community named Cuba. What does *cuba* mean in English?
A: Trough or tank.

Q: What famous southeastern New Mexico town was originally called Eddy after John and Charles Eddy?
A: Carlsbad.

Q: What town with an uncertain founding date, but probably 1740, has a Spanish name meaning Bethlehem?
A: Belén.

Q: John and Charles Eddy named Carlsbad. What other famous New Mexico town did they name in 1898 that is Spanish for "large cottonwood"?
A: Alamogordo.

Moriarty in central New Mexico routinely attracts Sherlock Holmes buffs.

Q: What town in southwest New Mexico was described, in 1882, as having "three newspapers, four stamp mills, two smelters, twelve saloons and three churches"?

A: Silver City.

Q: What distinction does Elizabethtown hold among the towns of New Mexico?

A: It was the first incorporated town in New Mexico and is now a ghost town.

Q: What two towns have recorded whole years in which there has been no days without frost?

A: Eagle Nest and Red River.

Q: The ghost town of Waldo was named after Henry L. Waldo. What important national appointment was given to him by President Ulysses Grant in 1876?

A: Chief justice of the New Mexico Supreme Court.

Q: What city's main street once had Christmas decorations of cardboard Santa Clauses carrying bags labeled "uranium"?

Grants once had cardboard Santa Clauses carrying bags marked uranium during the holidays.

A: Grants.

Q: Camino del Monte Sol, a street in what New Mexico city, was once described as "the street where those queer people built all their crazy houses. The mud-huts nuts"?
A: Santa Fe.

Q: North Mesa, South Mesa, Otowi Mesa, Kwage Mesa, Pajarito Mesa and Two-mile Mesa all have to be negotiated to get around in what town?
A: Los Alamos.

Q: It is believed the ancient Aztec emperor Montezuma enjoyed the healing hot springs of what present-day village?
A: Montezuma.

Q: What town was often referred to as the "Crossroads of the Out-laws" and "Satan's Paradise"?
A: Cimarron.

Q: What community boasts the southernmost ski area in the United

States?
A: Cloudcroft.

Q: Cloudcroft was started in the late 1890s as a resort for train excursions out of El Paso. What building housed the tourists and still survives for the same purpose today?
A: The Cloudcroft Lodge.

Q: In what community would you find Prince Tocom and Princess Kari during the Piñata Festival?
A: Tucumcari.

Q: Where did Buffalo Bill Cody meet with Annie Oakley to plan his "Wild West Show"?
A: The St. James Hotel in Cimarron.

Q: Who also stayed at the St. James while he sketched the nearby hills?
A: Frederic Remington.

Q: How many people have been killed in the notorious St. James Hotel?
A: Twenty-six.

Q: Where was New Mexico's first public high school founded in 1884?
A: Ratón.

Q: Continuously run for over 60 years, what claims to be the oldest rodeo in the United States?
A: The Fourth of July Rodeo in Ratón.

Q: Where is the oldest, privately owned horse racing track in New Mexico?
A: La Mesa Park in Ratón.

Q: In what year did the village of Angel Fire incorporate?
A: In 1986, it became New Mexico's 99th municipality.

Q: What was the town of Eagle Nest's original name?
A: Therma.

Q: What village was incorporated in 1976 as a bicentennial village?
A: Eagle Nest.

Q: The ranch of Luís María Cabeza de Vaca later became what town?

Rancho de las Golondrinas near Santa Fe is a living, Colonial New Mexico museum that often holds traditional events.

A: Las Vegas.

Q: In 1881, Galisteo Junction changed its name to what, after becoming the main connection from Santa Fe to the Atchison, Topeka & Santa Fe Railway?
A: Lamy.

Q: El Ortíz was the name of a hotel at Lamy built by what famous restaurateur?
A: Fred Harvey. It was also called the Lamy Harvey House.

Q: The old Pink Garter saloon in Lamy is now what popular restaurant?
A: The Legal Tender.

Q: In what village did the postmastership stay in the Santiago Martínez family for 68 years?
A: Truchas.

Q: Nine Indian Pueblos existed in what basin south of Santa Fe?
A: Galisteo.

Q: What family laid out the village of Galisteo?
A: The Ortíz family.

Q: What Colonial village museum near Santa Fe is a member of the "Living Historic Farms and Agricultural Museums Association" sponsored by the Smithsonian Institution?
A: El Rancho de las Golondrinas.

Q: Soldiers at Fort Union would often go to a village on the banks of the Mora River called Loma Parda for the purpose of boozing and frolicking with the many "ladies of the evening." Because of this, Loma Parda was nicknamed what?
A: Sodom on the Mora.

Q: What community is predicted to be the second largest city in New Mexico by the year 2000?
A: Rio Rancho, near Albuquerque.

Q: Albuquerque's population is what fraction of the entire state's population?
A: One-third.

Q: What town could at one time, claim to be the largest city west of San Antonio, Texas, was the site for Billy the Kid's trial and was the capital of the Confederate Territory of Arizona?
A: Mesilla.

Q: What were the White Elephant, the Red Baron, the Free and Easy and the Bucket of Blood?
A: Saloons in 1880s Albuquerque.

Q: In 1900, Glorieta was the big seller in Albuquerque. Who or what was Glorieta?
A: A locally brewed beer.

Q: According to the 1990 census what is the second most populous city in New Mexico?
A: Las Cruces.

Q: Where was the Gadsden Purchase signed?
A: La Mesilla.

Q: Who, in the 1930s, called Roswell "the prettiest little town in the West"?
A: Will Rogers.

The Plaza at La Mesilla was made a state monument in 1957.

Q: The Buddy Holly and Norman Petty Days was held in what town from Aug. 30 through Sept. 6, 1987?
A: Clovis.

Q: What New Mexico city beat out Dallas, Colorado Springs and Elmira, N.Y., in 1986 to become the national headquarters of the Soaring Society of America?
A: Hobbs.

Q: What town was originally founded in 1881 as New Chicago?
A: Deming.

Q: The town of Thoreau, probably named for Henry David Thoreau when the railroad established a station here, is pronounced how?
A: Through.

Q: Roswell's main street is very wide and was designed so for a purpose when the town was laid out by Van C. Smith in 1870. For what particular purpose was the street made so wide?
A: To accommodate large herds of cattle passing through town.

Q: Where can you find the Abó Underground School, called by the local chamber of commerce "probably the first underground school structure in the free world"?
A: Artesia.

Q: First named Riley's Switch, it was changed to honor the king of the Franks who converted to Christianity in A.D. 496. What town is it?
A: Clovis.

Q: What town manufactures more livestock feed than any town west of Kansas City, as well as having the largest grain-storage facilities in the state?
A: Clovis.

Q: What town, named for a likeness of Mary Magdalene in the nearby foothills, was at one time the largest cattle-shipping center of the Southwest?
A: Magdalena.

Q: A gas station owner on U.S. 60 near the Continental Divide became locally famous for the pies he baked and sold to customers. What is the town called today?
A: Pie Town.

Q: What is the main attraction to Pie Town today?
A: The huge outdoor sculpture by Walter de María called *The Lightning Field*.

Q: The village of San Ysidro was named for whom?
A: St. Isidore, the patron saint of farmers.

Q: The municipal buildings of Jémez Springs are heated by what method?
A: Geothermal heat.

Q: Jémez Springs was once quite a rowdy town with sheep wars, vigilante groups and gambling establishments. What law enforcement group once secretly headquartered itself in the Abousleman House?
A: The FBI.

Q: Cave openings that looked like porch arches gave the name to what town?
A: Portales.

Q: What village has been the home of Billy the Kid, Helen Hayes, Paul Horgan, Peter Hurd and Henriette Wyeth?
A: San Patricio, near Ruidoso.

Q: Dowlin's Mill became what town?
A: Ruidoso.

Q: Antelope Wells is an important stop in New Mexico for what reason?
A: It is a 24-hour port of entry to Mexico.

Q: Who founded the city of Santa Fe in 1610?
A: Pedro de Peralta, one of the provincial governors of New Mexico.

Q: The formal name for Santa Cruz is what?
A: Villa Nueva de Santa Cruz de los Españoles Mejicanos del Rey Nuestro Señor Carlos Segundo (New City of the Holy Cross of the Mexican Spaniards of Our Lord, King Charles II).

Q: What city calls itself the "City of Roses"?
A: Tularosa.

Q: What city's population suddenly quadrupled in the 1950s?
A: Alamogordo, due to the growth of the White Sands Missile Range.

Q: What town's chamber of commerce printed its population as "approximately 4,000 people within a 5-mile radius and three soreheads," and it also has the only bridge in Lea County?
A: Jal.

Q: What entire town was put up for sale in the 1970s?
A: Madrid.

Q: Was it sold?
A: No.

6

MINES
AND
MINERALS

One of the biggest industries in the state is mining. It plays a very important part in the state's economy and so it should be represented in any book about New Mexico.

Some believe there is still a treasure of gold hidden at Victorio Peak near White Sands.

Q: On what peak near White Sands is there rumored to be a lost treasure of gold?

A: Victorio.

Q: What important natural resource is found in the Permian Basin in southeastern New Mexico?

A: Oil.

Q: What village was considered the center of turquoise mining in New Mexico?

A: Cerrillos.

Q: The earliest records of gold mining by the Spaniards in New Mexico prior to 1680 indicate two areas of activity. One was at Cerrillos near Santa Fe and the other was where?

A: Near Taos.

Q: The Spanish began mining copper near Santa Rita, now the site of a large open pit copper mine, in what year?

A: 1804.

Q: In 1807, it was noted by Zebulon Pike that what mineral was being used as windows in Santa Fe?
A: "Flexible talc," probably mica.

Q: In 1828, placer gold was discovered in the Ortíz Mountains south of Santa Fe. What was so significant about this discovery?
A: It's considered the first important discovery of gold west of the Mississippi.

Q: For how long has turquoise been mined in New Mexico?
A: For at least 1,200 years.

Q: The name turquoise is French for what?
A: Turkish stone.

Q: Where is "the site of the most extensive prehistoric mining operations known on the American continent"?
A: Mount Chalchihuitl near Cerrillos in Santa Fe County.

Q: What has been claimed to remedy hernia, swellings, flatulence, dispepsia, insanity . . . cancerous sores, epilepsy and spleen?
A: Turquoise.

Q: During the Spanish Colonial period, there were two principal mining areas in New Mexico. Where were they?
A: Cerrillos and Santa Rita.

Q: According to legend, the "Lost Mines of The Aztecs" were lost to the world when the Indians filled in the shafts and tunnels after the Pueblo Revolt of 1680. Where are these mines, which are purported to be extremely rich in gold and silver?
A: In the mountains north of Taos.

Q: Why should a shepherd named José Francisco Ortíz hold a more prominent place in the annals of the West?
A: He made the first major gold discovery of the West in 1828, 21 years before it was found in California.

Q: It was reported that the gold mines of Dolores were abandoned in 1858. Why?
A: Because of Indian attacks.

Q: Why were mines around Santa Rita so dangerous to operate and were continually abandoned?
A: Indian attacks.

The ruins of Elizabethtown, once one of the largest gold mining towns in New Mexico.

Q: What did the Texas Confederates do with 300,000 pounds of Santa Rita copper left at Port Lavaca?

A: They used it in making cannons for the war.

Q: Where did one of the richest gold strikes in New Mexico occur in 1866?

A: Willow Creek Gulch in the Moreno Valley near modern-day Eagle Nest.

Q: One of the largest gold mining towns in New Mexico sprang up almost overnight, acquiring a population 7,000 in the 1870s, due to the discovery of gold on Willow Creek. What was its name?

A: Elizabethtown.

Q: Due to the scarcity of water to wash the gravel, a tremendous effort was put into building a ditch and aqueduct from the Red River into the Moreno Valley. How long was it?

A: Forty-one miles and it cost $210,000 to construct.

Q: What well-known person was a founder of the company that built the ditch?

A: Lucien Maxwell of the Maxwell Land Grant.

Q: Elizabethtown survived, as mining continued in the area, until when?
A: The 1940s.

Q: What particular group of men discovered gold in 1859 near Pinos Altos, just north of present-day Silver City?
A: The forty-niners returning from the gold strikes in California.

Q: What were the Red Bandanna, Ajax, French Henry, Thunder, Contention, Paragon, Bull-of-the-Woods, Puzzler and Little Jessie?
A: Gold mines of the Moreno Valley.

Q: What were the Turquoise City, Poverty Hollow, Bonanza City, Carbonateville and Purden's?
A: Lead and silver mining camps around Cerrillos.

Q: A small farm, named La Cienega de la San Vicente by its owners, was the site of what major mineral discovery in southwest New Mexico?
A: Silver. The "farm" is present-day Silver City.

Q: What mineral made boomtowns out of Kelly and Magdalena in the early 1870s?
A: Lead.

Q: What successful mining venture took place in the Petaca district of Río Arriba County in the 1870s?
A: The mining of mica.

Q: What unusual mineral (and rare in the Western Hemisphere) was found north of Silver City and mined with a modicum of success in the late 1870s?
A: Meerschaum.

Q: The town of Red River was laid out in 1894 due to the discovery of small deposits of gold, silver, lead and copper. One of the first corporate developers of copper in the area was a famous watch company from back East. What was it?
A: The Waltham Watch Co.

Q: What mineral product gained success in the 1880s and 1890s at Ojo Caliente in Río Arriba County?
A: Mineral water. In 1892 to 1893, 46,000 gallons were marketed.

A cottonwood tree once served as the jail for the mining town of Mogollón.

Q: White Oaks was laid out in 1880 after the discovery of important lode and placer gold ores in the area. Lincoln County Sheriff Pat Garrett was there when what famous outlaw escaped from Garrett's jail in Lincoln?

A: Billy the Kid.

Q: In the 1880s, Socorro saw so much mining activity that it was thought it would become the mining center of New Mexico. It didn't, but what institution was established there?

A: New Mexico Institute of Mining and Technology.

Q: What "rip-roaring mining camp," from 1885 to 1900, accounted for most of New Mexico's fairly high gold output?

A: Mogollón.

Q: At one time, Mogollón had no jail. What did they do with lawbreakers?

A: Chained them to a cottonwood tree.

Q: The mill for the mines above Whitewater Canyon was supplied with water through an 18-inch pipeline installed along the steep northern wall of the canyon. To make repairs, the workmen walked the pipe. What did they call it?

A: The Catwalk.

Q: Is the pipe still there?
A: No, but a metal grid walkway has been installed so that present-day visitors can make the same journey.

Q: What is considered to be New Mexico's finest "ghost" gold camp today?
A: Mogollón.

Q: It has been said of a mine at Lake Valley that, "Out of this hole came one of the richest bodies of silver in the history of mining." Also, much of this was horn silver, so pure that it was sawed and cut into blocks. What's the name of this spectacular mine?
A: The Bridal Chamber.

Q: What present-day, well-known ghost town near Santa Fe was once a thriving coal mine and became nationally famous for its elaborate annual Christmas display?
A: Madrid.

Q: What is an estimate of the total dollar amount of all minerals mined in New Mexico prior to 1900?
A: $100,000,000.

Q: What single mineral contributed the most to this figure?
A: Coal, at $40,000,000.

Q: What decade saw the largest silver production in the history of New Mexico?
A: 1880-1890.

Q: What important event took place in Eddy County in 1909?
A: The first oil well in New Mexico was drilled.

Q: What was first discovered in New Mexico at the Navajo Reservation in San Juan County in 1882?
A: Oil.

Q: Known as Bravo Dome, where is one of the largest natural carbon dioxide deposits in the entire world?
A: Near Clayton.

Q: What engineering feat is located at 10,500 feet on Baldy Mountain near Eagle Nest?

A: A five-mile mining tunnel through the mountain.

Q: On the road west of Albuquerque can be seen the scarred remains of the Anaconda Jackpile Mine. Before it closed in 1981, it was the largest open pit mine of what mineral in the world?
A: Uranium.

Q: What are Pecos Valley diamonds?
A: Chunks of quartz crystals that are unique to the area around Roswell.

Q: What is known as the state police diamond, which many officers have inlaid in their whistles, guns and wristwatches?
A: Turquoise.

Q: What did Paddy Martínez, a Navajo sheep rancher, discover near Grants in 1950 that launched a whole industry?
A: Uranium.

The Grants Museum of Mining features mining memorabilia.

58

7

A NAME
YOU MAY
RECOGNIZE

Because of its appeal, New Mexico has drawn to it the famous and infamous. What's that name again?

Truchas is the location of the film, The Milagro Beanfield War, *also a popular New Mexican novel by John Nichols.*

Q: What famous inventor came to the mountains near Santa Fe in the early 1890s to prospect for gold?
A: Thomas A. Edison.

Q: Edison erected a plant near Dolores to extract gold from gravel using what method?
A: Static electricity.

Q: The Santa Fe Ring interested many people in New Mexico land speculation. A friend of Jerome Chafee, one of the Ring's leaders, was among them. Who was he?
A: George M. Pullman, builder of sleeper cars.

Q: In the 1920s, what famous psychologist visited the New Mexico Pueblo Indians and was told by an Indian man that white men were mad because they thought with their heads instead of their hearts?
A: C.G. Jung.

Q: What famous publisher took a lease on the Santa Rita Copper Mine in 1897?

A: William Randolph Hearst.

Q: What well-known New York family, whose name became associated with decorative lamps, owned the American Turquoise Co. in Cerrillos?
A: The Tiffanys. The Tiffany Mine still exists.

Q: Who flew from Lordsburg to Santa Fe via El Paso in 1927?
A: Charles A. Lindbergh.

Q: The Western novel *Frontier Caravan* was written at the St. James Hotel in Cimarron in 1929. Who was the author?
A: Zane Grey.

Q: These people all have something in common: Clay Allison, Davy Crockett II, Elfego Baca, Bob Ford, Jesse James, Buffalo Bill Cody, Lew Wallace, Bat Masterson, Annie Oakley, Frank Butler. What is it?
A: They all stayed at the St. James Hotel in Cimarron.

Q: The Pecos Pueblo National Historic Site has a visitors' center and museum. What actress and benefactress provided the funds to build them?
A: Greer Garson.

Q: William Matthewson became the first person to go by this nickname because he provided meat to starving pioneer families. What was this famous moniker?
A: Buffalo Bill.

Q: Who pulled up on a flatbed wagon in Golden, placed a gramophone on it and played cylinder records for the crowd?
A: Thomas A. Edison.

Q: Where did Lew Wallace, territorial governor of New Mexico, finish his book *Ben Hur*?
A: At the Palace of the Governors in Santa Fe.

Q: A famous Western artist once visited a rancher near Horse Springs looking for landscapes to paint. Who was he?
A: Frederic Remington.

Q: A chapter in a very famous book was devoted entirely to Edmund G. Ross, a Kansas senator whose vote saved President Andrew Jackson from being impeached and who later became the territorial governor of New Mexico. He eventually retired in Albuquerque

Cartoonist Bill Mauldin, who gained fame during World War II, grew up in High Rolls near Alamogordo and lives in Santa Fe.

and is also buried there, but what's the name of the book in which he was featured?

A: *Profiles In Courage* by John F. Kennedy.

Q: What famous hotel tycoon was born and raised in San Antonio, N.M.?
A: Conrad Hilton.

Q: What internationally famous artist lived near Abiquiú?
A: Georgia O'Keeffe.

Q: In what town did D.H. Lawrence once live?
A: Taos.

Q: At Washington's National Zoo, what New Mexico-born animal got so much fan mail that he was assigned his own zip code (20252)?
A: Smokey Bear.

Q: What Football Hall of Fame hero was chairman of the investors who financed the opening of the Taos Ski Valley in 1955?
A: Doak Walker.

Q: Norman Petty from Clovis, became world famous in music circles and once visited London at the request of Paul McCartney. Who is he?

A: The man who recorded Buddy Holly's first hits and launched Holly on the road to success. Petty also recorded Roy Orbison, Waylon Jennings, Jimmy Gilmer and the Fireballs, Chita Rivera and Brad Maule—all in Clovis.

Q: What well-known ABC newsman graduated from New Mexico Military Institute in Roswell?

A: Sam Donaldson.

Q: What famous auto racing family lives in Albuquerque?

A: The Unsers: Bobby; Al; Robby; and Al Jr.

Q: What former Dallas Cowboy football star runs the New Mexico Gallery of Photography and Art in La Mesilla?

A: Bob Lilly.

Q: What former U.S. senator from New Mexico walked on the moon?

A: Harrison Schmitt.

Q: In 1932, who dedicated the airport at Lordsburg?

A: Charles A. Lindbergh.

Q: High Rolls, on U.S. 82 between Cloudcroft and Alamogordo, was the boyhood home of what famous cartoonist?

A: Bill Mauldin.

Q: Fort Selden, built as a defense against the Apaches, lasted for 25 years. Who was the famous son of one of the post commanders that lived at the fort?

A: Gen. Douglas MacArthur.

Q: Who said, "If you ever go to New Mexico, it will itch you for the rest of your life"?

A: Georgia O'Keeffe.

8

ARTS AND ENTERTAINMENT

New Mexico has been written about extensively during recent years in books and periodicals throughout the country. One of the qualities of the state is that it has drawn to it over the years many creative, talented people. What is it that makes New Mexico so attractive to this group of people? Maybe some of the answers will be found as you read the questions and answers in this section.

Q: Rancho Alegre near Santa Fe is used for what?
A: It's an old Western town movie set.

Q: The Pit is well-known in New Mexico. What is it?
A: The University of New Mexico Lobos basketball arena.

Q: What film did Robert Redford direct in northern New Mexico?
A: *The Milagro Beanfield War.*

Q: In the 1920s Josef Bakos, Fremont Ellis, Walter Mruk, Willard Nash and Will Shuster became the founding fathers of the art movement in Santa Fe. What did they call themselves?
A: Los Cinco Pintores (the five painters).

Q: What is the one main quality about New Mexico that most artists claim brought them here?
A: The light.

Q: A well-known New Mexico artist, Peter Hurd, had a famous artist as a father-in-law. Who?
A: N.C. Wyeth, whose son, Andrew, learned tempera painting from Peter Hurd.

Q: There used to be a bookstore in Santa Fe called the Villagra Book Shop, named after Gaspar Pérez de Villagrá. Who was he?
A: A Spanish poet whose epic poem *Historia* extolled the deeds of the Spanish conquerors of New Mexico.

Q: What were *Los Titeres* in Colonial New Mexico?
A: Traveling puppet shows.

Q: What has been described as, "Its likes can be seen nowhere else in the world for it comes out of the very soul of native New Mexico"?
A: *Santero* art (saint-related sculpture and painting called *bultos* and *retablos*).

Q: Among state film commissions, what unique position does New Mexico's Film Commission hold?
A: It was the first, in 1968.

Q: The internationally famous Santa Fe Opera was established in what year?
A: 1957.

Q: What opera by Igor Stravinsky was performed at St. Francis Auditorium in Santa Fe and was conducted by the composer himself?

The courtyard of the Palace of the Governors in Santa Fe.

A: *The Rake's Progress.*

Q: A famous book by Willa Cather was written about Archbishop Jean
Baptiste Lamy, the first U.S. Catholic priest in New Mexico. What's
its name?
A: *Death Comes for the Archbishop.*

Q: For what art form is the prestigious Tamarind Institute at the University of New Mexico noted?
A: Printmaking.

Q: The Albuquerque-Santa Fe-Taos area is third only to the East
Coast and West Coast in the sales of what commodity?
A: Art.

Q: What are *Yei, Yeibichei* and *Teec Nos Pos?*
A: Navajo weaving designs.

Q: Which Indians are considered the masters of basket making?
A: The Apaches.

Q: What New Mexico village is considered the heart of Spanish blanket weaving?
A: Chimayó.

Q: Ancient pottery found in southern New Mexico dates pottery making in the state from about what year?
A: A.D. 200.

Q: One of the most renowned potters of recent times lived and worked at San Ildefonso Pueblo. She specialized in black pots with a high sheen. What's her name?
A: María Martínez.

Q: María and Julian Martínez of San Ildefonso Pueblo rediscovered the technique of making black pottery. What was the main method they did during the firing of the pot?
A: They covered it with powdered dung.

Q: Santa Clara Pueblo potters use a certain technique which has become their trademark. What is it?
A: Sgraffito (scratchings).

Q: What specific form of clay work was popularized in the 1960s by Helen Cordero of the Cochiti Pueblo?
A: Storyteller figurines.

Q: During the middle of the 19th century, an Indian named Atsidi' Sani became the first in a long line of well-known craftsmen. What skill did he learn from the Spaniards?
A: Silversmithing.

Q: What internationally known photographer lived in Tesuque and was known for his beautiful color photos of nature?
A: Eliot Porter.

Q: Georgia O'Keeffe and D.H. Lawrence, among other artists, made homes here due mainly to the encouragement of what woman and patroness of the arts?
A: Mabel Dodge Luhan of Dodge motorcar fame. Her home can be seen in Taos.

Q: Georgia O'Keeffe moved to her home near Abiquiú permanently in 1949. What had happened three years earlier that allowed her to make such a change in her life?
A: The death of her husband, famed photographer Alfred Stieglitz.

Peculiar antics and costumes are part of the popular and traditional
Spanish Matachines *Dance.*

Q: One photographer's most recognized photo is titled *Moonrise, Hernández, New Mexico.* What world-renowned photographer took this picture?

A: Ansel Adams.

Q: What was D.H. Lawrence describing in the following quote, ". . . the spirits of the men go out of the ether, vibrating in waves from the hot, dark, intentional blood. . . ."?

A: A Taos Pueblo dance.

Q: What is *Los Matachines*?

A: A popular, traditional Spanish dance.

Q: What New Mexican wrote the 1980 Tony Award-winner *Children Of A Lesser God*, which had its debut at New Mexico State University in Las Cruces?

A: Mark Medoff.

Q: A beloved New Mexican, Cleofes Vigil of San Cristóbal, is a Fellow with the National Endowment for the Arts and has performed his skill on several visits to Washington, D.C. What is Cleofes' talent?

A: He is a master storyteller.

Q: New Mexican Oliver La Farge wrote a novel called *Laughing Boy*. What was so special about this book?
A: It won the 1929 Pulitzer Prize.

Q: A presumably wealthy man from Boston, named George Coluzzi, lived on the edge of Santa Fe and would sculpt large rocks he brought down from the surrounding hills then return them to their place of origin. He was an artist who lived in a peculiar dwelling for a rich man. What was it?
A: A cave.

Q: In what New Mexico book and popular movie starring Richard Thomas was the character of George Coluzzi depicted?
A: *Red Sky At Morning.*

Q: What famous author, when looking out across the countryside south of Santa Fe, said, "It looks like eternity"?
A: William Carlos Williams.

Q: What Pulitzer Prize-winning journalist once wrote about living in Albuquerque, "We have seen sunrises so violently beautiful they were almost frightening and I'm only sorry I can't capture the sunsets and the thunderstorms and the first snows on the Sandías, and take them east and flaunt them in people's faces"?
A: Ernie Pyle.

Q: Bert Phillips and Ernest Blumenschein are famous in northern New Mexico for doing what?
A: Establishing an art colony in Taos in 1898.

Q: *The Brave Cowboy* and *Fire on the Mountain* were two books about New Mexico made into movies. What author and environmental activist wrote them?
A: Edward Abbey.

Q: Who is Mark Nohl?
A: His beautiful photographs appear in almost every issue of *New Mexico Magazine* and his work has received awards as far away as Maine.

Q: Who has published over 20 books on Southwest history, especially concerning New Mexico; has won the Golden Spur Award from the Western Writers of America; was instrumental in gaining National Historic Trail status for the Santa Fe Trail and is consid-

María Benitez in classic flamenco form.

ered an expert on the history of that trail; and in 1986 won the Texas Western Press C.L. Sonnichsen Book Award for his *Murder On The Santa Fe Trail?*

A: Marc Simmons.

Q: What Santa Fe resident and New Mexican native has been called "a young Andre Segovia, one of the world's finest classical guitarists," and has played with some of the country's finest symphonies?

A: Ruben Romero.

Q: New Mexican María Benitez dazzles Santa Fe audiences every summer with her tremendous talent that has been praised by the top performers in her profession. What does María do that is so wonderful to watch?

A: Flamenco dancing.

Q: What author of *The House At Otowi Bridge* laughingly called herself an octogeranium when she turned 80?

A: Peggy Pond Church.

Q: Who was Peggy Pond Church's father?
A: Ashley Pond.

Q: What did he do?
A: He ran the Los Alamos Boy's Ranch before the government took it over for the Manhattan Project in the early 1940s.

Q: A film, considered a landmark in international cinema but has no dialogue or story, was the creation of Santa Fean Godfrey Reggio. What is the film, with photography by Ron Fricke and music by Philip Glass?
A: *Koyaanisqatsi.* A Hopi Indian word for "life out of balance."

Q: In September 1987, The Santa Fe Film Festival presented one of the most comprehensive tributes ever mounted for an American filmmaker. Who was honored by the festival which among other events, showed about 30 of his films?
A: John Huston, who died just a few days before the event.

Q: What Santa Fe artist, who had a gallery on Canyon Road, was at one time a justice of the peace in Santa Fe and Truchas, and gained national attention as the only judge in America to hold court in an art gallery?
A: Bill Tate, who died in 1987.

Q: What heavy metallic dinnerware, started as a small business near Santa Fe, has become famous nationwide for its beautifully designed bowls, plates and trays?
A: Nambé Ware.

Q: In 1987, the Southwest Ballet Company of New Mexico was "allowed" to perform what ballet, a privilege granted to only a few companies by the estate of choreographer Eugene Loring?
A: *Billy The Kid*, music by Aaron Copland.

Q: Commissioned in 1941 by an El Paso couple, the Pottery House, as it was called by its designer, was only recently built in the hills of Santa Fe. Who was the architect?
A: Frank Lloyd Wright.

Q: Agnes Morley Cleaveland, one of the state's most popular and colorful figures, wrote what book about her adventures as a young girl growing up in the cattle country of the Datil Mountains during the late 19th century?
A: *No Life For A Lady.*

The outdoor Santa Fe Opera is world famous.

Q: What would you most likely witness at the Greyhound Arena?
A: Basketball at Eastern New Mexico University in Portales.

Q: After whom or what was the popular Paolo Soleri outdoor theatre at the Santa Fe Indian School named?
A: Its architect, Paolo Soleri.

Q: Where will you find tailgaters enjoying a picnic before the "big show"?
A: The Santa Fe Opera.

Q: Joe Cisneros, a real-life miner in northern New Mexico, was the model for what fictional character created by John Nichols for his novel *The Milagro Beanfield War*?
A: Joe Mondragon.

Q: Who filmed *Indian Day School*, probably the first movie made in New Mexico, in 1898?
A: Thomas A. Edison.

9

HIGHWAYS AND BYWAYS

F rom the Santa Fe Trail to Route 66, New Mexico's roads are just as notorious as some of its citizens. See if you don't agree.

The historic and renovated Plaza Hotel in Las Vegas, N.M.

Q: In 1831, in Missouri, what medium of exchange was preferred over the American dollar?
A: The Mexican silver *peso*, due to the Santa Fe Trail traffic.

Q: In 1846, when New Mexico first became part of the United States, a woman crossed the Santa Fe Trail and became the first American female to write a trail journal. Who was she?
A: Susan Shelby Magoffin.

Q: The inhabitants of what New Mexico town were described by Susan Magoffin in 1846 as "those wild looking strangers"?
A: Las Vegas.

Q: Who is credited with establishing the Santa Fe Trail?
A: William Becknell.

Q: Who persuaded the U.S. government to mark the Santa Fe Trail in 1824?
A: Missouri Sen. Thomas Hart Benton.

Q: How long did it take early travelers on the Santa Fe Trail to cross the Ratón Pass?

A: Up to five days.

Q: To what honored occupation did the *arriero* belong?
A: Muleteer.

Q: The Santa Fe Trail actually became an extension of what already existing road of commerce that had prospered in New Mexico for almost 200 years?
A: *El Camino Real de Tierra Adentro.*

Q: In 1783, regular mail delivery was inaugurated on *El Camino Real*. How often did the deliveries occur?
A: Four times a year.

Q: How much did it cost to mail a letter?
A: One-half *peso.*

Q: What two cities did *El Camino Real* connect?
A: Santa Fe and Chihuahua, Mexico.

Q: *El Camino Real* (Royal Road) was also known by another name. What was it?
A: The Chihuahua Trail.

Q: Who was Josiah Gregg and what was his contribution to the Santa Fe Trail?
A: He was an early trader on the trail and wrote *The Commerce of The Prairies*, considered must reading for any Santa Fe Trail buff.

Q: What was unusual about the completion, in 1880, of the Atchison, Topeka & Santa Fe Railway from Chicago to the Río Grande?
A: It bypassed Santa Fe.

Q: The situation was corrected by installing a track connecting Santa Fe to the AT&SF at what town near Santa Fe?
A: Lamy.

Q: How much were passengers charged per mile on the Overland Mail and Express stage which took them to Santa Fe from railheads in Colorado?
A: Twenty cents.

Q: Chicosa Lake, near Roy, was once a watering hole on what famous cattle trail?

Although not indigenous, domestic camels once used to trek across New Mexico, but were dropped in favor of the horse.

A: The Goodnight-Loving Trail.

Q: What major stage road went through southwest New Mexico?
A: The Butterfield Stage Route.

Q: What trail left Santa Fe for Colorado and Utah and into California?
A: The Old Spanish Trail.

Q: What large Eastern city's name was prominently displayed on the first steam engine that drove into Santa Fe in 1880?
A: Boston.

Q: What did a man named A.W. Whipple do that helped open up communication in the Southwest?
A: He established the first road from Albuquerque to California.

Q: In 1857, what unusual form of transportation traveled along Whipple's route?
A: Camels.

Q: Who initiated the plan to provide the Army with camels?

Ruts from wagons traveling along the Santa Fe Trail are still visible on the eastern plains.

A: Jefferson Davis, who was then the U.S. Secretary of War, but later became the president of the Confederacy.

Q: Besides being the route of *El Camino Real*, Interstate 25 south of Santa Fe is also called what?
A: The Pan American Central Highway.

Q: The San Juan extension of the Denver & Río Grande Railroad is today known as what?
A: The Cumbres & Toltec Scenic Railroad.

Q: What railroad in New Mexico is a registered national historic site?
A: The Cumbres & Toltec Scenic Railroad.

Q: What is the "Clayton Complex" and why is it significant?
A: It is an important area of the Santa Fe Trail and wagon ruts are still visible.

Q: The building now known as the Santa Fe Trail Museum and Historical Society in Springer was once what important structure?
A: The Colfax County Courthouse.

Q: The Santa Fe Trail provided access to a large trade clientele. A man could pay $150 for a wagon in Missouri and get how much for it in Santa Fe?
A: $700.

Q: What did the command "Stretch out! Stretch out!" do?
A: It started the wagons on the road across the Santa Fe Trail.

Q: How much did Richard Lacy "Uncle Dick" Wootton charge each wagon to use his toll road over the Ratón Pass in the 1860s?
A: $1.50.

Q: There was one group of people that Uncle Dick never charged to use his toll road. Who were they?
A: Indians.

Q: Scurvy was a major disease of travelers on the Santa Fe Trail. What cured that disease when they got to New Mexico?
A: Chile.

Q: How did chile cure scurvy?
A: It has a large amount of vitamin C.

Q: Giovanni Juan María Agostini, a Italian religious mystic, had both a cave and a peak named after him along the Santa Fe Trail. What are they called?
A: Hermit's Cave and Hermit's Peak.

Q: In 1850, the first stage line traveled the Santa Fe Trail. What was the fare from Independence, Mo., to Santa Fe?
A: $250 one way.

Q: How many days were scheduled to make the trip?
A: Twenty-five.

Q: By 1863, they could make the trip in how many days?
A: Fourteen.

Q: The AT&SF followed what old route?
A: The Santa Fe Trail.

Q: Why didn't the AT&SF main line go to Santa Fe?
A: Because of steep grades.

Q: Central Avenue in Albuquerque, going east and west through town, used to be part of a more well-known thoroughfare. What

Once a rambunctious stop along the Santa Fe Railway, The Castañeda Hotel in Las Vegas is now a shell of its old self.

was this nationally known romantic byway?

A: Route 66.

Q: What is Route 66 known as today?
A: Interstate 40.

Q: The Castañeda Hotel, still standing in Las Vegas, was built to serve the patrons of the Santa Fe Railway. Who had it built?
A: Fred Harvey, of the Harvey Girls fame.

Q: What is U.S. 60 going west from Socorro nicknamed because it rises 2,000 feet in only 16 miles?
A: The elevator.

Q: At times U.S. 70 south of Alamogordo is closed to all traffic. Why?
A: Because of missile testing at White Sands Missile Range.

Q: Interstate 10 between Las Cruces and Deming roughly parallels what old trail?
A: The Butterfield Stage Route.

Q: The Butterfield route went from St. Louis to San Francisco via El Paso. How often was there a rest stop for change of horses or riders?

A: Every nine miles.

Q: A daily route from Torrance to Roswell was the first of what?

A: The first U.S. mail route for rural delivery by automobile in the nation.

Q: U.S. 82 just west of High Rolls features, among other things, the only what in the state?

A: The only highway tunnel.

Q: This same road descends 4,500 feet in 16 miles and offers a spectacular, panoramic view of what geologic wonder?

A: White Sands.

White Sands National Monument continues to awe its visitors.

10

NOTORIOUS FELLOWS

New Mexico seems to have had more than its fair share of bad guys and infamous characters. Who are those guys?

William Bonney became world famous as Billy the Kid.

Q: In what town did Henry McCarty, a.k.a. William Antrim, William Bonney and Billy the Kid, live with his mother and go to school?
A: Silver City.

Q: From what still-preserved building did Billy make his famous escape, killing two deputies?
A: The Lincoln County Courthouse (the old Murphy-Dolan Store of Lincoln County War fame).

Q: Who wrote a highly fictionalized biography of Billy the Kid?
A: Pat Garrett.

Q: Myra Ellen Jenkins exclaimed, "I nearly dropped my teeth when I saw it." When he discovered it, Dale Bullock reported, "I couldn't believe what I was seeing." What were they talking about?
A: One of only two known photographs of Billy the Kid.

Q: Where did Sheriff Pat Garrett first capture Billy the Kid on Dec. 23, 1880, after an all-day battle?
A: Stinking Springs.

Q: Pat Garrett and Billy the Kid were once friends before Garrett became sheriff of Lincoln County. What was Garrett's occupation when he and Billy the Kid were on better terms?
A: He was a bartender at Beaver Smith's saloon in Fort Sumner.

Q: After Fort Sumner was abandoned in 1868, Lucien Maxwell bought it from the government. He enlarged the officers' quarters to make a 20-room house for himself. What momentous event took place in this house in July 1881?
A: Pat Garrett shot Billy the Kid.

Q: Where is Sheriff Pat Garrett buried?
A: Las Cruces.

Q: Where is Billy the Kid buried?
A: Fort Sumner.

Q: Where did Wyatt Earp and John Henry "Doc" Holliday wind up, one week after they were forced to leave Tombstone, Ariz.?
A: Albuquerque.

Q: Who at one time operated a dental office in Las Vegas?
A: Doc Holliday.

Q: In 1882, a famous lawman ran a gambling hall in Old Town of Albuquerque. Who was he?
A: Wyatt Earp.

Q: What famous Missouri outlaw worked on the railroads in New Mexico to hide out from the law?
A: Jesse James.

Q: What famous gunman played a role in the Colfax County War?
A: R.C. "Clay" Allison.

Q: Why did Clay Allison shoot Pancho Griego at the St. James Hotel in Cimarron in 1875?
A: Griego had accused Allison of being in a lynch mob that had caused the death of Cruz Vega, a friend of Griego.

Q: What horrible act did Allison perform in 1870 after another lynch mob he was part of, in Elizabethtown, hanged a suspected killer?
A: He beheaded the corpse and rode to Cimarron with the head on a pike.

Q: Not long after that Allison was challenged by another gunfighter,

The Dorsey Mansion is dramatically different from typical New Mexican architecture.

Chunk Colbert. Allison promptly shot him in the head. What were these two doing when the fight broke out?

A: They were having dinner together at a Colfax County inn.

Q: Again in Colfax County, Allison had a dispute with another rancher and they had arranged for a knife fight at a later date, when Allison returned from a trip to Texas. But what happened?

A: Allison accidentally fell under a moving wagon and was run over the neck by one of its wheels, killing him July 1, 1887, near Pecos, Texas.

Q: One of the tales concerning Clay Allison has him dancing on the bar of the St. James Hotel saloon in Cimarron. But what was so unusual about that?

A: He danced nude.

Q: Who was once described as "the one man, who more than any other, dominated New Mexico's political and business affairs for fifty years"?

A: Thomas B. Catron.

Q: A University of Missouri graduate and an officer in the Confederate Army, Catron became a leader of what influential political machine in New Mexico?
A: The Santa Fe Ring.

Q: In the late 1800s Catron held a distinction among landlords. What was it?
A: He was the largest private landholder in the United States.

Q: George Curry, later to become the territorial governor of New Mexico, was at one time involved in a major battle of the Colfax County War as a member of The Vigilantes. He was prosecuted by a well-known Santa Fe attorney who was unable to travel to Cimarron or Springer for years afterward because of threats to his life by the Vigilantes. Who was this lawyer?
A: Thomas B. Catron.

Q: What successful lawyer for land grant owners during the Colfax County War made so much money from this venture that he retired from law and became a world famous paleontologist?
A: Frank Springer.

Q: Frank Springer once owned a newspaper that boasted an unusually long name. What was it?
A: *Cimarron News and Elizabeth City Railway Press and Telegraph.*

Q: The nephew of a famous frontiersman with the same name, once went on trial in Cimarron for murdering three men and later was shot and killed by a posse when he resisted arrest for disturbing the peace. What was his name?
A: David Crockett.

Q: What colorful New Mexican was a candidate for the U.S. House of Representatives at the Sept. 28, 1911, Republican Convention held in Las Vegas? His fame was established in Reserve during a gunfight.
A: Elfego Baca.

Q: In 1880, Henri Lambert owned and operated the St. James Hotel. Before coming to New Mexico, Lambert worked for Gen. Ulysses Grant and later Abraham Lincoln. What did he do for them?
A: Cook.

Q: Stephen W. Dorsey, a former U.S. senator from Arkansas and once involved in a major mail fraud, was a great defender of the Maxwell Land Grant. He ran 22,000 head of cattle on 12,000-plus acres near the grant property. His ranch house was quite elaborate and is still known today as what?

A: Dorsey Mansion.

Q: The notorious outlaw Black Jack Ketchum robbed the Colorado and Southern passenger train three times in a row in the exact same spot when it slowed going up a slope near what town?

A: Folsom.

Q: On the third time the authorities caught Black Jack and hanged him at Clayton. What happened when he made the big fall?

A: His head snapped so hard he was decapitated.

Q: Mysterious Dave Mather, a cohort of Wyatt Earp and Doc Holliday and of the same ilk, was charged with robbery and then became a lawman in what town?

A: Las Vegas.

Q: What outlaw is considered one of New Mexico's most horrendous criminals for leading a band of up to 40 bandits, which he called *La Sociedad de Bandidos de Nuevo Méjico*, and for murdering his wife and others?

A: Vicente Silva of Las Vegas.

Q: Port Stockton, an outlaw from the Lincoln County War, came to what town and was made a peace officer?

A: Bloomfield.

Q: What happened to Stockton?

A: He returned to a life of crime while still a peace officer, but was eventually killed by the local sheriff.

Q: Wayne Brazel was accused of shooting and killing what famous lawman near Organ on Feb. 29, 1908?

A: Pat Garrett.

Q: What happened to Brazel?

A: He admitted to the killing, but was later acquitted in a trial.

Q: Albert B. Fall owned Tres Ritos Ranch north of Tularosa and it was here that discussions took place that created a national scandal in 1921 about the Elks Hill Reserve in Wyoming. What was this better known as, and eventually caused Fall to spend six months in prison?

A: The Teapot Dome Scandal.

Q: Charles G. Kusz once published a paper in Manzano for several years after the Civil War titled *The Gringo and the Greaser*. What happened to this publisher?

A: He was assassinated.

Vicente Silva, of Las Vegas notoriety, was an upstanding citizen by day and cold-blooded killer by night.

11

A NATURAL STATE

This section asks about everything from Carlsbad Caverns to La Fiesta de Santa Fe, but mostly it is about the natural wonders of the state.

Legend states that Shiprock delivered the Navajo people to safety in northwestern New Mexico from unfriendly people.

Q: Near Ácoma is a large area of land called El Malpais, which means bad country in Spanish. What is El Malpais?
A: A huge lava flow.

Q: Called Turquoise Mountain by the Navajos, what prominent mountain was later renamed for a U.S. general following the Mexican War in 1846?
A: Mount Taylor, after Gen. Zachary Taylor.

Q: At times, when the rain is sufficient, what lakes can be the largest natural lakes in the state?
A: The salt lakes on Laguna del Perro near Willard and Estancia.

Q: Due to their proximity to the salt beds, the Spanish called the Gran Quivera, Abó and Quarai Indian villages by what collective name?
A: The Salinas Pueblos.

Q: The late Federico Cisneros, who owned the property of the Abó Pueblo ruins, sold it to the state for $1 and agreed to care for it. He was put on the payroll and when the federal government took over

Angel Peak near Bloomfield sits in the Garden of Angels.

the site in 1981, Federico became what?
A: The oldest ranger in the U.S. Park Service.

Q: What is the state's largest county?
A: Catron.

Q: What attracts visitors to Aztec?
A: The Aztec Ruins National Monument.

Q: The Aztec Ruins National Monument is really a misnomer. Why?
A: Early settlers believed they were occupied by Aztec Indians. They weren't.

Q: Who occupied these dwellings?
A: The Anasazi, probably of the Chaco Canyon culture.

Q: South of Bloomfield, what prominent mountain can be seen for miles around and stands in the middle of what is known as the Garden of The Angels?
A: Angel Peak.

Q: What happens to the Continental Divide as it bisects the Plains of San Agustín?
A: It goes in an east-west direction.

Q: The caprock of eastern New Mexico has rims with corrugated cliffs formed like an *estacada* or stockade, and is the most likely source for what name given to the vast plains that cover the eastern edge of the state?
A: Llano Estacado or Staked Plains. Other sources claim that the name has to do with actual stakes being driven into the ground for various reasons.

Q: In the 1880s, the whole of northern Lea County had only one huge cottonwood tree. What was it used for?
A: A hanging tree for horse thieves.

Q: What mountain range in New Mexico is among the few in the country that runs east and west and has no major streams?
A: The Capitán Mountains.

Q: Believed to be the youngest lava flow in the continental United States, the Valley of Fires Recreation Area lies just a few miles west of what town?
A: Carrizozo.

Q: In what mountain range would you find Buzzard Canyon, Strychnine Draw, Freezeout Canyon and Last Chance Canyon?
A: The Guadalupe Mountains.

Q: Fourth of July Canyon near Tajique features something unique in New Mexico. What?
A: Maple trees.

Q: What famous natural landmark is located near Farmington?
A: Shiprock.

Q: What four states can you stand in at the same time in the Four Corners area?
A: Arizona, Colorado, New Mexico and Utah.

Q: What famous ranch is located near Cimarron and is inhabited by boys?
A: Philmont Scout Ranch.

Q: What well-known chapel is located near Eagle Nest?
A: The DAV Vietnam Veterans Memorial Chapel.

Chaco National Historical Park once was a thriving cultural center of the Anasazi Indians.

Q: Where is the world's longest tramway?
A: On Sandía Peak near Albuquerque.

Q: What natural landmarks are prominent on the mesa west of Albuquerque?
A: A series of extinct volcanoes.

Q: Cochití Dam south of Santa Fe, holds back what body of water?
A: The Río Grande.

Q: What is an *acequia madre*?
A: A main irrigation ditch, or "mother ditch."

Q: San Miguel Mission in Santa Fe is noted for what?
A: It is believed to be the second oldest church in the United States.

Q: A Spanish explorer named Juan de Jaramillo made an important geographic discovery while traveling with Coronado in what is now New Mexico. What did he find?
A: The Continental Divide.

Q: What river was once known as "Coronado's River of La Señora"?
A: The Río Grande.

Q: The name of a major mountain range of the Southern Rockies that turn red at sunset came into being at the beginning of the 19th century mainly because of the *Penitentes* who practiced their beliefs at the foot of its peaks. What's its name?
A: Sangre de Cristo (Spanish for blood of Christ).

Q: What are the Lower Sonoran, Upper Sonoran, Transition, Canadian, Hudsonian and Arctic Alpine?
A: The six life zones (out of the seven possible in the world) of vegetation in New Mexico.

Q: Comprising 2,458,505 acres, what is the largest national forest in New Mexico?
A: The Gila National Forest in southwest New Mexico.

Q: Ruins of the Anasazi culture can be seen in what canyon in northwest New Mexico?
A: Chaco Canyon.

Q: One of the first areas the Pueblo Indians settled along the Río Grande was in Frijoles Canyon on the Pajarito Plateau. What is the area known as today?
A: Bandelier National Monument.

Q: During what period of time was this area occupied?
A: From the 1200s to the 1500s.

Q: New Mexico has an area of 121,660 square miles, placing it in what position in size among the states?
A: Fifth.

Q: The Palace of the Governors in Santa Fe is the oldest capitol building in the United States. What is unique about the current state capitol building?
A: It is the newest capitol building in the United States.

Q: For how long was the Palace of the Governors actually used as the capitol building of New Mexico?
A: For almost 300 years.

Q: In 1886, what historical event took place regarding the Palace of the Governors?

The burning of Zozobra highlights La Fiesta de Santa Fe.

A: Its use as a capitol building was discontinued when a new building was erected south of the Santa Fe River.

Q: What happened to this new capitol building six years later?
A: It mysteriously burned to the ground.

Q: What does the annual La Fiesta de Santa Fe commemorate?
A: The ritual repossession of New Mexico by Diego de Vargas in September 1692.

Q: This three-day event features a Friday night burning of Zozobra. What is Zozobra?
A: A 40-foot moving, growling and monstrous puppet that represents Old Man Gloom.

Q: La Fiesta de Santa Fe is one of the oldest public festivals in the United States. What event brings it to an end?
A: A somber, candlelight procession that makes its way to a large, lit cross on top of Fort Marcy Hill, the site of New Mexico's first established military fort.

Q: Red Bluff Reservoir in southern Eddy County holds what geographic distinction in New Mexico?
A: It is the lowest point in New Mexico at 2,841 feet.

Q: What ancient pueblo ruin is located the farthest east?
A: Pecos.

Q: The modern-day Santa Clara Pueblo Indians south of Española claim their ancestors lived here hundreds of years ago. They still own and maintain what remarkable example of ancient pueblo and cliff dwellings?
A: Puyé Cliff Dwellings.

Q: Where, in February, can you witness the departure of sandhill cranes and whooping cranes for their summer homes in Idaho?
A: Bosque del Apache National Wildlife Refuge near Socorro.

Q: What well-known natural landmark is located north of Tesuque right along U.S. 84-285, making it a popular tourist stop?
A: Camel Rock.

Q: Valle Grande, a huge grassy valley in the Jémez Mountains near Los Alamos, is actually what kind of geographic formation?
A: A volcanic caldera.

Q: Capulín Mountain is a prominent landmark in the northeastern plains of New Mexico. What is so distinctive about it?
A: It is a perfect volcanic cone.

Q: From the top of what mountain near Ratón can you see 200 miles over four different states?
A: Capulín Mountain.

Q: More than 500 dinosaur tracks can be seen 12 miles north of what town?
A: Clayton.

Q: When were these tracks discovered?
A: In 1982 by an amateur paleontologist.

Q: When these tracks were made over 100-million years ago, what was this area?
A: The shore of the modern-day Gulf of Mexico.

Q: What is considered one of the most beautiful historic churches in the Southwest and painted by some of the country's finest artists

San Francisco de Asis Church in Ranchos de Taos is arguably one of the most photographed locations in New Mexico.

and photographed by top-notch photographers?
A: San Francisco de Asis Church in Ranchos de Taos.

Q: What engineering marvel completed in 1965 is a big tourist attraction located on the Río Grande near Taos?
A: The Río Grande Gorge Bridge, the second-highest suspension bridge in the United States.

Q: Located north and east of Tularosa one can find over 500 examples of what?
A: Ancient Indian rock writings or petroglyphs.

Q: What are the largest gypsum dune deposits in the world called?
A: White Sands National Monument.

Q: At sunset, from early May through October, what unique experience can you witness at Carlsbad Caverns?
A: Bat flights.

Q: The largest lake in New Mexico, Elephant Butte, was formed by damming the Río Grande near Truth or Consequences. How long,

Elephant Butte Lake is named after an adjoining massive rock formation that resembles a giant elephant.

north to south, is Elephant Butte?
A: Forty-five miles.

Q: Where can you find the village of Fra Cristóbal?
A: Beneath the waters of Elephant Butte Lake.

Q: Scuba divers consider Blue Hole, an artesian spring 87 feet deep and 60 feet across, one of the finest spots to enjoy their sport in the entire state. Where is Blue Hole?
A: Near Santa Rosa.

Q: What does "riding the box" mean in northern New Mexico?
A: Rafting through a certain white-water section of the Río Grande.

Q: Several people have jumped off Sandia Peak near Albuquerque and survived. Why?
A: It is a popular place for hang gliding.

Q: An area north of Chaco Canyon is one of the world's most important and strikingly beautiful fossil resources. What name has this preserved wilderness area been given?

A: The Bisti Badlands.

Q: Bottomless Lakes State Park east of Roswell was New Mexico's first what?
A: State park, established in 1933.

The Bisti Badlands resemble another world.

12

SOMETIMES WE DIDN'T GET ALONG

There have been many conflicts in New Mexico during its history, including troubles over land grants, water rights, outlaws, politics, Indians, cattle, the Civil War, territorial possession by the United States and even statehood itself. Some of these conflicts are significant, and these are the ones that the following questions cover.

Gen. Lew Wallace in his Indiana study. Later as governor of New Mexico, he finished Ben Hur *in the Palace of the Governors in Santa Fe. (Museum of New Mexico photo, Neg. No. 40340.)*

Q: In what famous war did Billy the Kid fight on what he considered the side of the law?
A: The Lincoln County War.

Q: Who made a deal with Billy the Kid for a pardon in trade for information about some killings during the Lincoln County War?
A: Territorial Gov. Lew Wallace.

Q: Why was Billy later arrested?
A: For killing Sheriff William Brady.

Q: The men riding on the Tunstall-McSween side of the Lincoln County War called themselves The Regulators. Who sometimes led this group?
A: Billy the Kid.

Q: What New Mexican town is noted for a famous raid by Pancho Villa into the United States?
A: Columbus.

Q: What was the name of the Army post in Santa Fe?

A: Fort Marcy.

Q: What happened to Fort Marcy in the early part of 1862?
A: It was occupied by the Confederate Army under Gen. Henry Sibley.

Q: Where was the capital of the Confederate Territory of Arizona in 1861?
A: Mesilla.

Q: Was New Mexico aligned with the Union or the Confederacy during the Civil War?
A: The Union.

Q: What was the original intention of the taking of New Mexico by the Confederacy?
A: To open up the Confederate states to gold-rich California.

Q: What significant battle drove the Confederates from New Mexico?
A: The Battle of Glorieta Pass.

Q: Why was the Battle of Glorieta Pass so important?
A: It stopped the western advance of the Confederacy.

Q: What was the major obstacle facing U.S. Surveyor General William Pelham when he arrived in Santa Fe in 1854?
A: Sorting out over 1,000 land grants.

Q: What were Cebolla, Conejos, Beck, Cuchilla, San Cristóbal, Cienequilla, Mora and Los Luceros?
A: New Mexico land grants.

Q: Eventually, more than 80 percent of the Spanish land grants would wind up in the hands of what particular group of men?
A: American lawyers.

Q: Who described these lawyers as "sharp, shrewd Americans . . . possessed of some local lore and with a large amount of cheek and an unusual quantity of low cunning and astuteness"?
A: E.G. Ross, a former governor of the New Mexico territory.

Q: What was the largest and most disputed land grant?
A: The Maxwell Land Grant.

Q: The disputes over the Maxwell Land Grant led to violence in northeastern New Mexico. This trouble came to be known as what?

Frank Springer, left, near the Rito de los Frijoles in 1915 with Santiago Naranjo, Kenneth Chapman and Carlos Vierra. (Museum of New Mexico photo, Neg. No. 28087.)

A: The Colfax County War.

Q: Oscar P. McMains, who was opposed to the grant, was charged with the murder of Cruz Vega whom McMains suspected of killing his friend, Franklin J. Tolby. In what profession were both Tolby and McMains?
A: They were Methodist ministers.

Q: In 1885, the grant men of Ratón hired the brother of a notorious gunman to form a militia against the anti-grant crowd. Who was this man?
A: James Masterson, brother of "Bat."

Q: The anti-grant men rebelled against this militia idea and formed their own group to run Masterson out of the state. What did they call their group?
A: The Vigilantes.

Q: George Curry, later to become governor of the Territory of New Mexico, was a Vigilante. His brother, John, and two other Vigilantes were killed in a grant-related shootout in which George

took an active role and was later jailed for his participation. In what town did this happen?
A: Springer.

Q: What incident touched off the violence in the Colfax County War?
A: The murder of Franklin J. Tolby.

Q: What group was suspected of arranging the murder?
A: The notorious Santa Fe Ring.

Q: Why were they suspected?
A: Because Tolby opposed them.

Q: Tolby opposed them over what issue, which was also the main impetus for the problems of Colfax County?
A: The Maxwell Land Grant.

Q: Lucien Maxwell had sold the grant to a group of investors who called their company what?
A: The Maxwell Land Grant and Railway Co.

Q: Due to a questionable survey, the investors managed to expand the grant's acreage from 96,000 acres to almost how many acres?
A: Two million.

Q: This display of greed, along with Tolby's murder, started the crusade of what man in the fight against the grant?
A: Tolby's friend, Oscar P. McMains.

Q: McMains managed to gather evidence for Tolby's murder against Cruz Vega. What happened to Vega?
A: He was killed by a lynch mob.

Q: Who led the mob?
A: O.P. McMains, although he was not present during the actual killing.

Q: Manuel Cardenas, who was implicated in the murder of Tolby by Cruz Vega, was arrested and confessed that three prominent citizens of Cimarron, with ties to the Santa Fe Ring, were also involved. But before a grand jury could hear the whole story what happened?
A: Cardenas was shot in the head, while in custody at the door of the county jail.

Q: What rumor circulated about O.P. McMains and Clay Allison?

Clay Allison did what many modern politicians would like to do—he threw the press of unfavorable publicity in the river.

A: That they were partners in tracking down the killers of Tolby.

Q: Because an article in favor of the Santa Fe Ring appeared in the Cimarron newspaper, what did Allison do in January 1876?
A: He ransacked the office and threw the press into the Cimarron River.

Q: A grand jury investigating the deaths of Tolby, Vega and Cardenas convened in Taos. O.P. McMains was indicted for the murder of Cruz Vega and put on trial at Mora. What was unusual about the verdict?
A: McMains was found "guilty in the fifth degree" and fined $300. No one knew what the fifth degree was and the jury didn't specify the crime.

Q: In 1878, a plot by the New Mexico territorial governor, Samuel Axtell, to murder Frank Springer, Clay Allison and others for their opposition to the Santa Fe Ring was uncovered. What happened to Axtell?
A: He was removed from office by President Rutherford B. Hayes.

Q: Who replaced Gov. Axtell?
A: Gen. Lew Wallace.

Q: For almost 20 years O.P. McMains and others fought the owners and their exaggerated claims of the Maxwell Land Grant. Did McMains win his legal battles?
A: No. In the late 1800s the U.S. Supreme Court ruled against him.

Q: For a period of about one month, from March to April 1862, where did the Executive Department of the territorial government conduct business?
A: Las Vegas.

Q: Why?
A: The Confederate Army had invaded and seized Santa Fe.

Q: In their invasion into New Mexico, how did the 2nd Texas Mounted Rifles take Fort Bliss without a fight?
A: The fort had been abandoned by the U.S. forces.

Q: With all the other forts in the southern part of the territory being abandoned, including forts Stanton, Fillmore and Buchanan, what one fort stood its ground and helped hold off the Confederates?
A: Fort Craig.

Q: Confederate Gen. H.H. Sibley came to the territory to organize several Texas regiments that became known as what?
A: The Army of New Mexico.

Q: What was happening at Fort Union at this time?
A: The fort was abandoned and rebuilt about a mile farther out onto the plains.

Q: What was unusual about the new Fort Union?
A: It was an earthwork in the shape of a star.

Q: During this period of unrest, what outside force gave both the Union and Confederate generals cause for concern?
A: Indian attacks.

Q: Who led the 1st Volunteer Regiment at Fort Craig?
A: Kit Carson.

Q: Which side won the Battle of Valverde near Fort Craig?
A: The Confederates.

Fort Union in northeastern New Mexico once protected travelers on the Santa Fe Trail.

Q: Who did Yankee officers blame for the superior Union forces' loss?
A: Col. E.R.S. Canby. He had retreated instead of fighting it out.

Q: The specific engagement known as the Battle of Glorieta, was initially dominated by the Confederates. How did this become such a decisive victory for the Union?
A: Destruction of the Confederate supply train behind their supply lines "without the loss of one Union soldier."

Q: In his retreat, Confederate Gen. Sibley's forces had a serious skirmish south of Albuquerque with the Union forces under Col. Canby who had moved north from Fort Craig. Who won?
A: Canby.

Q: In his continued retreat down the west bank of the Río Grande, Gen. Sibley's troops were always in sight of immediate destruction. Why?
A: Canby's superior forces were parallel to him on the east bank of the river.

Q: Why didn't Col. Canby cross the river and destroy the Rebels?

A: He said he didn't want to have to provide for the prisoners that would be taken. He was later criticized for his lack of action.

Q: What finally broke the river standoff?
A: Sibley's troops sneaked out during the night and went west 100 miles out of their way to avoid conflict.

Q: The beaten, starving Confederates finally showed up at Fort Bliss the first day of May 1862. What news drove the Confederates, every man for himself, back to San Antonio?
A: That the "California Column," who had been alerted about the Confederates trying to take the West, were fast approaching from Southern California.

Q: In 1848, the Treaty of Guadalupe Hidalgo brought an end to what war?
A: The Mexican War.

Q: The Franciscan friars of the 1600s, while trying to force Christianity on the Indians, destroyed kivas and demolished kachinas. What happened as a result?
A: The Pueblo Revolt of 1680.

Q: During the rebellion, who were the first to be killed by the Indians?
A: Catholic priests and brothers.

Q: In what pueblo is the 1680 Pueblo Revolt said to have started?
A: Tesuque.

Q: What was the last Indian pueblo to yield to Spanish power in 1699?
A: Ácoma.

Q: In 1714, the Spanish rulers of New Mexico actually debated whether or not the Indians should be allowed to do what?
A: Paint themselves.

Q: In 1837, the Revolutionary Movement was created. What revolution was this?
A: New Mexicans against the Mexican government.

Q: What was the reason for the Taos Rebellion in January 1847?
A: Many New Mexico natives, both Mexican and Indian, did not want to be taken over by the United States.

Q: The first fort in New Mexico was named after the secretary of war

Ácoma Pueblo is also known as Sky City.

during the Mexican War. Who was he?

A: William L. Marcy.

Q: What was unusual about the 9th and 10th Cavalries, "The Buffalo Soldiers," under Col. Edward Hatch who garrisoned New Mexico and gallantly fought the great Apache Chief Victorio?

A: All the enlisted men were black.

Q: In 1888, the Good and Lee families fought a war in Tularosa that was bloodier than the neighboring Lincoln County War. What was it over?

A: Cattle.

Q: Where did the last hostile land action by foreign troops within the continental United States take place?

A: Columbus.

Q: When Pancho Villa raided Columbus in 1916, who did President Woodrow Wilson send to drive him out?

A: Gen. John J. Pershing.

Q: What caused an international crisis during Pershing's campaign?
A: He took his troops into Mexico.

Q: Two extremely important U.S. military firsts regarding transportation took place during this same campaign. What were they?
A: The first military use of aircraft and motorized vehicles.

Q: About how many New Mexicans served in the armed forces during World War I?
A: 17,000.

Q: During World War II, a group consisting mostly of New Mexicans of the 200th Coast Artillery were the victims of an infamous death march. Where did this take place?
A: Bataan, in the Philippine Islands.

Q: Where was Camp Luna, the World War II training camp for the 200th Coastal Artillery, many of whose members died on Bataan?
A: Las Vegas.

Q: A state government building in Santa Fe is named in honor of those members of the 200th Coast Artillery. What's it called?
A: The Bataan Memorial Building (it was the former capitol).

Q: A specialized group of New Mexico Navajo Indians became famous during World War II. Why?
A: The Navajo Code Talkers used their native tongue to transmit radio messages. The Japanese were unable to translate the Navajo language.

Q: How many New Mexicans served in the armed forces during World War II?
A: 60,000.

Q: A riot occurred in the streets of Mesilla in 1871, killing nine men and wounding 50 others. What two groups fought each other in this conflict?
A: Republicans and Democrats.

Q: What happened in Tierra Amarilla on June 5, 1967?
A: The Río Arriba County Courthouse raid.

Q: As with many conflicts in New Mexico's history, what issue was the cause of the raid?
A: Land grants.

Q: Who led the raid?
A: Reies López Tixerina, a.k.a. "The King Tiger."

Q: What was the name of the group he led?
A: Alianza Federal de Mercedes (Federal Alliance for Land Grants).

Q: Two men were shot, including a state policeman. Several people were taken hostage and the courthouse ransacked. What was the purpose of all this violence?
A: Specifically, to free some companions and to take into custody the district attorney, Alfonso Sanchez. Generally, to demonstrate the determination and seriousness of the Alianza.

Q: How did the state immediately respond to this incident?
A: It sent National Guardsmen with tanks and even anti-aircraft guns to hunt down the 20 or so raiders.

Q: Who said, ". . . the land is ours. The documents prove it. Justice is with us. Law is with us. God is with us. We are members of the Holy Race, *Hidalgos*"?
A: Reies López Tixerina.

Q: Did Tixerina achieve the goal of returning the land grants to their rightful owners?
A: No.

Q: Besides land grants, what is another reason for conflicts among New Mexicans?
A: Water rights.

13

20TH-CENTURY MISCELLANEOUS

S ome facts and trivia about New Mexico won't fall into nicely fitted categories. The following questions are somewhat of a miscellaneous nature, but do handle subjects that fall into a time from the turn of the century to modern-day New Mexico.

Pecos National Monument was abandoned by the Pecos Indians in favor of Jémez Pueblo to the northwest in the 1830s.

Q: What famous site is located in the Jornada del Muerto?
A: Trinity (the first atomic bomb explosion).

Q: Where were captured German V2 rockets taken to after World War II?
A: White Sands.

Q: In 1938, what did Oklahoma oilman Waite Phillips do with part of his huge ranch in northeastern New Mexico?
A: He donated it to the National Council of the Boy Scouts of America. It is known today as the Philmont Scout Ranch.

Q: Philmont Scout Ranch's main headquarters and a museum are today open to the public and it is located south of what town?
A: Cimarron.

Q: Both the Pecos State Monument and Coronado State Monument were created in what year?
A: 1935. (Pecos has since become a national historical park.)

Q: What were Need, Weed and Lingo in 1918?

A: U.S. post offices.

Q: Near Alamogordo in 1956, Malcolm McGregor's land was condemned and became U.S. property. For what purpose?
A: A missile-firing range.

Q: Who once noted about Los Alamos, "The scientists have been saying for years, 'Give us the world and we'll remake it.' Well, here it is. And isn't it bloody awful!'"?
A: British author J.B. Priestley.

Q: A Nigerian newspaper editor by the name of Cletus Xywanda once visited the city of Santa Fe and from his own personal experiences made what statement about the city, which must be true since it attracts an inordinate amount of creative people to it?
A: "Santa Fe celebrates the individual."

Q: In 1961, in Lincoln, invitations were sent out and a reception was held to honor Miss Lois Telfer. Why was Miss Telfer so honored?
A: She was the last surviving relative of Billy the Kid.

Q: Kaiser's Store of Elizabethtown in 1909 had these entries in its ledger: "By work on ranch; by gold; by check." What did they signify?
A: Means of bill payment.

Q: On Aug. 27, 1908, Sarah Rooke became a heroine by staying at her post in Folsom to warn others of the impending disaster in which she died. What happened?
A: A flood. Sarah was a telephone operator.

Q: In 1950, the governor's chauffeur, 6-foot, 11-inch Ingram B. Pickett, was pushed by those in power into the state Corporation Commission race as a vote splitter but won the election. Pickett had once worked in motion pictures as what?
A: A Keystone Cop.

Q: Built in Ratón in 1929 and now the home of International State Bank, what was the name of this hotel before it was changed to the Yucca Hotel during World War II?
A: The Swastika Hotel.

Q: Why was it called the Swastika?
A: Because it bore images of the swastika, an ancient Indian symbol for good luck.

Q: What happened on the Pajarito Plateau on April 15, 1943?
A: The formal opening of the Los Alamos National Laboratory, then

Double Eagle II makes its historic flight.

known as the Manhattan Project.

Q: The address at 109 E. Palace in Santa Fe became very important in 1943. Why?

A: It was where Manhattan Project personnel "checked in."

Q: Ácoma Pueblo, the "Sky City," sits atop a high cliff and could not be reached by modern automobiles until 1957 when what unlikely group improved and paved the road to the top?

A: A movie production company.

Q: What did Ben Abruzzo, Maxie Anderson and Larry Newman, three "high-flyin'" New Mexicans do in August 1978 that enthralled the world?

A: They were the first to cross the Atlantic in a balloon they called Double Eagle II.

Q: Double Eagle II can be viewed where?

A: At the Smithsonian Institution.

Q: Greg MacAleese, in 1976, was an Albuquerque policeman who started a program that has mushroomed nationwide and now you hear about it almost every night on local TV news programs all over the country. What is it?

A: Crime Stoppers.

Q: During the 1930s, the "Father of Rocketry" continued his experiments in New Mexico. Who was he?

A: Robert H. Goddard.

Q: On Oct. 5, 1977, the Rubio family of Lake Arthur became famous and a shrine is now located at their home because an image of Jesus Christ appeared to Mrs. Rubio. On what did the image appear?

A: A flour tortilla.

Q: In November 1944, the settlement of Tolar was completely flattened. What catastrophe caused this destruction?

A: A munitions train exploded leveling the town with flying shrapnel and train parts.

Q: What happened near Elida in 1913 that made the railroad tracks so slick that the trains couldn't run?

A: A grasshopper infestation.

Q: What name did the rangers give to a small bear cub that survived a forest fire and later became Smokey Bear?

A: Hot Foot Teddy.

Q: In 1906, the community of Ancho had a brick factory and trainloads of brick from here went to rebuild what destroyed city?

A: San Francisco.

Q: Each year between the 1920s and 1941, Transcontinental Airlines (now TWA) would reroute their flights to fly over Madrid at night for what reason?

A: So passengers could see the spectacular Christmas lights display that made the town famous.

Q: A famous treasure discovered in 1937 by Milton C. "Doc" Noss, but later rehidden by him, was brought up during the Watergate Hearings by John Dean and featured in *Time*, *Newsweek* and "60 Minutes." It was in litigation involving F. Lee Bailey and caused a dispute between the U.S. Army (it's located on the White Sands Missile Range) and the State of New Mexico. This famous treasure, supposedly worth billions, is reputedly still buried and goes by the name of its location. What is it?

A: The Treasure of Victorio Peak.

14

SUPERLATIVES

There are some things that only New Mexico can boast about.

Radio telescopes send signals to the wide, blue sky at the Very Large Array complex near Socorro.

Q: The oldest apple orchard in the United States is claimed to be in what New Mexican village?
A: Manzano (apple tree in Spanish).

Q: William Manderfield and T.J. Tucker founded one of the oldest newspapers in the Southwest. Which one?
A: *The Santa Fe New Mexican.*

Q: New Mexico, as a territory, held a distinction among other territories in the history of the United States. What was it?
A: It was a territory for more than 60 years, longer than any other in the 48 contiguous states.

Q: The Museum of International Folk Art in Santa Fe holds a distinction among museums. What is it?
A: The world's largest museum of folk art.

Q: What is perhaps the oldest road still in use in the United States, having once been an Indian trail into the Sangre de Cristo Mountains and is now noted for its art galleries?
A: Canyon Road in Santa Fe.

Q: El Llano Estacado (The Staked Plains) in southeast New Mexico lays claim to what geographical distinction?
A: It includes some of the flattest surfaces in the world.

Q: The orchard at the Stahman Farms near Las Cruces is said to be the largest of its kind in the world. What do they grow?
A: Pecans.

Q: What is considered to be the richest archaeological locale in North America?
A: Chaco Canyon National Historical Park in northwest New Mexico.

Q: Only California and the highlands of Central America have a greater variety of what life form than New Mexico?
A: Mammals.

Q: The Sacramento Peak Observatory at Sunspot near Cloudcroft is unique in the world. Why?
A: It is the world's largest, most sophisticated solar observation telescope.

Q: Where is the richest quarter horse race in the United States held?
A: Ruidoso Downs.

Q: On the Plains of San Agustín, west of Magdalena, stands the world's largest radio telescope. There are 27 antennas each 80 feet in diameter and 6 stories high. What is this complex, seen in the opening of the film *2010*, called?
A: The VLA (Very Large Array).

Q: Between 1870 and 1871, John Chisum was credited with having the largest holdings in the world of what commodity?
A: Cattle.

Q: What has been described as having "produced more evidence about early North American mammoth hunters than all other sites combined?
A: Blackwater Draw near Clovis.

15

NEW MEXICO TODAY

Taos Pueblo probably has been inhabited for more than 700 years.

Q: What is one of the main cash crops in New Mexico that is not usually associated with the state?
A: Cotton.

Q: Some New Mexico school districts include what special days in their holiday calendars?
A: Pueblo feast days.

Q: All food that is considered traditionally New Mexican contains at least one of three ingredients. What are they?
A: Corn, beans or chile.

Q: A hominy soup spiced with red chile and containing pork is a very popular New Mexican dish. What is it called?
A: *Posole* (poh-SOH-leh).

Q: What are *hornos* (OR-nohs)?
A: The beehive-shaped, adobe ovens closely associated with pueblos.

Q: Experts agree that no other state in the union, except perhaps Louisiana, enjoys what, that is as singular and pervasive as that

of New Mexico?
A: Its cuisine.

Q: More acres of what food crop are farmed in New Mexico than in any other state?
A: Chile.

Q: Chile is one of the two state vegetables (*frijoles* [beans] being the other). What's in error with this designation?
A: Chile is technically a fruit.

Q: What are *ristras* (REE-strahs)?
A: Long strings of clustered red chile. They are made to dry chile, but are popular because of their decorative value.

Q: Chiles actually cool the body. How?
A: They dilate the blood vessels and open sweat pores.

Q: Robert Sanchez, the current archbishop of the Roman Catholic Church in New Mexico, holds a distinction among his predecessors. What is it?
A: He is the first archbishop who is a native-born New Mexican.

Q: What well-known Eastern Indian religion has its Western headquarters near Española?
A: The Sikhs.

Q: What well-known, popular Indian powwow has been held every August for the past 58 years?
A: The Gallup Inter-tribal Indian Ceremonial.

Q: What's the most popular form of native architecture in New Mexico?
A: Pueblo Revival.

Q: What are *vigas* (VEE-gahs)?
A: The log beams on the ceilings of adobe buildings that sometimes protrude to the outside.

Q: What's the type of architecture that was introduced into the territory after the occupation by the United States in 1846?
A: Territorial.

Q: What New Mexican culinary delicacy is a *cabrito* (cah-BREE-toh)?
A: A roasted young goat.

The St. James Hotel in Cimmaron saw more than its share of gunfire.

Q: Room No. 18 at the St. James Hotel in Cimarron is notorious for what?

A: A ghost occupies it.

Q: The Ernest Thompson Seton Library is located at the Philmont Scout Ranch. Who was he?

A: An author, naturalist and artist who was the first "chief scout" of the Boy Scouts of America.

Q: Ed Sitzberger, a Los Alamos scientist, and his then-wife Pat did something in 1985 that contributed to the history of New Mexico. What did they do?

A: They restored and reopened the St. James Hotel in Cimarron.

Q: Albuquerque's International Balloon Fiesta holds what distinction?

A: The largest hot-air balloon gathering in the world.

Q: How many hot-air balloons can be seen flying over Albuquerque during the fiesta?

A: More than 500.

Q: The memorabilia-filled home of what beloved Pulitzer Prize-winning journalist is now a public library in Albuquerque?
A: Ernie Pyle.

Q: About 10,500 rock drawings can be seen at Indian Petroglyph State Park just west of what city?
A: Albuquerque.

Q: What are New Mexico 6-4, Sandia, Rio Grande, Nu-Mex and Big Jim?
A: The most common, commercially produced chiles of New Mexico.

Q: What did Will Rogers call the Inter-tribal Indian Ceremonial?
A: "The greatest Indian show on earth."

Q: Where is the Home of the World's Richest Duck Race?
A: Deming.

Q: What has Luna County Courthouse Park been renamed?
A: Deming Duck Downs.

Q: What is the parade called that takes place during the races?
A: The Tournament of Ducks Parade.

Q: What is the main organizer of this annual event called?
A: The Chief Quacker.

Q: Where is the world's most complete display of nuclear weapons?
A: At the National Atomic Museum at Kirtland Air Force Base in Albuquerque.

Q: What event in Albuquerque draws an overall crowd that numbers greater than the state's population?
A: The New Mexico State Fair.

Q: What state park has the most visitors?
A: Elephant Butte State Park.

Q: At 6,250 acres, it claims to be the world's largest campus. What school is it?
A: New Mexico State University in Las Cruces.

Q: In Albuquerque, what is known as "The Big I"?
A: The spaghetti bowl tangle of highways where I-40 intersects with I-25.

Many Americans still consider New Mexico a foreign country.

Q: What animal, usually associated with South America, is enjoying an increased popularity in New Mexico?

A: The llama.

Q: A continuing and very popular humorous feature of the *New Mexico Magazine* is "One of Our Fifty is Missing." What does this regular column feature?

A: True anecdotes of mostly New Mexican residents' experiences with government agencies, universities, businesses, the media, maps, individuals, etc., that mistake New Mexico as a foreign country or that it is the Republic of Mexico.

Q: What is the San Cristóbal Ranch north of Taos?

A: It is the ranch given to D.H. Lawrence's wife, Frieda, by her friend Mabel Dodge Luhan.

Q: Lea County, in southeast New Mexico, is known more for oil than for cowboys, yet it has produced more champions in what sport than any other county in the United States?

A: Rodeo.

Q: In 1880, New Mexico was producing 905,000 barrels of this annually. In 1983 the production was only 20,000 gallons. What beverage is this?
A: Wine.

Q: Four Albuquerque residents, in 1986, found the remains of a dinosaur skeleton 60 miles northwest of Albuquerque. Evidence shows it belonged to the largest creature ever to walk the face of Earth, being 120 feet long and weighing as much as 13 bull elephants. What quite appropriate scientific name was given to this gargantuan beast?
A: *Seismosaurus* (Latin for the earth shaker).

Q: Who was Ernie Blake?
A: He started and ran the world famous Taos Ski Valley.

Q: Al's Run at Taos Ski Valley (one of the most difficult runs there) was named for Al Rosen, a significant contributor to the success of the area who suffered a massive heart attack in 1961 and was told never to ski again. He did, however, continue skiing for 23 years . . . with his oxygen tank and mask! What was Al's profession?
A: He was a physician in Taos.

Q: As refreshment (for those skiers who find them), what did Ernie Blake hide under the giant spruces of Taos Ski Valley?
A: *Porones*, small glass vessels filled with martinis.

Q: What is known as "West Point of the West"?
A: New Mexico Military Institute in Roswell.

Q: What New Mexico elementary school team won the 1984 National Elementary Chess Tournament?
A: Pojoaque (poh-whah-keh).

Q: To avoid confusion in the rest of the United States, what did former Gov. Garrey Carruthers order to be added to New Mexico license plates in 1987?
A: U.S.A.

Q: A New Mexico wine, the St. Clair Sauvignon Blanc Reserve 1984, won a gold medal at an international competition in Geneva, Switzerland. Where is the St. Clair Winery?
A: Near Deming.

Q: The famous Randall Davey home in Santa Fe, now owned by the

Audubon Society, was once what?

A: A sawmill.

Q: The John Chisum Ranch near Roswell is owned by what university which maintains the ranch as it was in the 1870s?

A: Cornell University.

Q: Melrose annually presents a unique kind of rodeo. What's so different about it?

A: It's an all-female rodeo.

Q: In late November and early December, where can you see between 30,000 to 75,000 snow geese concentrated on one lake?

A: At the Bitter Lake National Wildlife Refuge near Roswell.

Q: Why was a luxury resort near Santa Fe named Bishop's Lodge?

A: It was once the residence of Archbishop Jean Baptiste Lamy.

Q: What is trinitite?

A: Desert soil fused into glass by the blast of the first atomic explosion at Trinity Site.

Rodeo competition remains a staple in New Mexico.

Sources.

1. *The Gunfighter.* (Time-Life Books, 1974.)
2. *Ghost Towns and Mining Camps of New Mexico* by James E. and Barbara H. Sherman. (University of Oklahoma Press, 1975.)
3. *Ranchers, Ramblers and Renegades* by Marc Simmons. (Ancient City Press, 1984.)
4. *Inventing Billy the Kid* by Stephen Tatum. (University of New Mexico Press, 1982.)
5. *Down the Santa Fe Trail and Into Mexico: The Diary of Susan Shelby Magoffin, 1846-1847.* (Yale University Press, New Haven, Conn., 1962.)
6. *New Mexico Past & Present* by Richard N. Ellis. (University of New Mexico Press, 1971.)
7. *Taos to Tóme: True Tales of Hispanic New Mexico* by Marc Simmons. (Ancient City Press, 1978.)
8. *On The Santa Fe Trail* by Marc Simmons. (University Press of Kansas, 1986.)
9. *A Journey Through New Mexico History* by Donald R. Lavash. (Bishop Publishing Co., Portales, N.M., 1972.)
10. *Four Fighters of Lincoln County* by Robert M. Utley. (University of New Mexico Press, 1986.)
11. *Pioneering in Territorial Silver City* edited and annotated by Helen J. Lundwall. (University of New Mexico Press, 1983.)
12. *The Maxwell Land Grant* by William A. Keleher. (University of New Mexico Press, 1942.)
13. *Along the Santa Fe Trail*, essay by Marc Simmons. (University of New Mexico Press, 1986.)
14. *The Indian Frontier of the American West, 1846-1890* by Robert M. Utley. (University of New Mexico Press, 1984.)
15. *The Commerce of the Prairies* by Josiah Gregg, 1844. (University of Nebraska Press, 1967.)
16. "Summer Visitor's Guide." (*The Taos News*, 1987.)
17. "Summer Enchantment." (*Sangre de Cristo Chronicle*, 1987.)
18. "The Enchanted Circle." (*New Mexico Business Journal*, Community Profile, Special Section, April 1987.)
19. "Official Albuquerque Visitor's Guide." (Albuquerque Convention and Visitor's Bureau, 1987-88 Edition.)
20. *Mapa Histórico de Taos.* (Kiwanis Club of Taos, 26th Edition, 1874-1985.)
21. "Your Host . . . New Mexico." *The Tourist Key to the Land of Enchantment.* (Albuquerque, July 1987.)
22. *Eagle Nest—Gateway to the Enchanted Circle.* (A Winter 1986 Publication of the Eagle Nest Chamber of Commerce.)

23. "On Assignment." (KNME-TV Channel 5, July 1, 1987.)
24. *Historic New Mexico Calendar 1986* by Holt Priddy, 1985.
25. *The Great Taos Bank Robbery and Other Indian Country Affairs* by Tony Hillerman. (University of New Mexico Press, 1973.)
26. *Albuquerque Journal*, June 7, 1987.
27. *The Spell of New Mexico*, edited by Tony Hillerman. (University of New Mexico Press, 1976.)
28. Santa Fe National Forest Map. (U.S. Department of Agriculture Forest Service, 1975.)
29. *Santa Fe Trail Trivia*, compiled by Leo E. Oliva and Bonita M. Oliva. (Western Books, Woodston, Kan., 1987.)
30. *Mysterious Dave Mather* by Colin Rickards. (The Blue Feather Press for The Press of the Territorian, Santa Fe, N.M., 1968.)
31. *Mountain Villages* by Alice Bullock. (Sunstone Press, Santa Fe, 1981.)
32. *New Mexico Magazine.* Nov. 1978; Feb. 1980; Mar. 1980; May 1980; July 1982; Mar. 1984; April 1984; May 1984; Oct. 1984; Feb. 1985; April 1985; Aug. 1985; Oct. 1985; Sept. 1986; Nov. 1986; Dec. 1986; Feb. 1987; Mar. 1987; April 1987; and June 1987.
33. *Santa Fe Style* by Christine Mather and Sharon Woods. (Rizzoli International Publications, New York, 1986.)
34. "The Spirit of Santa Fe." (*National Geographic Traveler*, [summer] 1987.)
35. *New Mexico Place Names*, edited by T.M. Pearce. (University of New Mexico Press, 1965.)
36. KOB News, Channel 4, June 4, 1987.
37. *Historical Atlas of New Mexico* by Warren A. Beck and Ynez D. Haase. (University of Oklahoma Press, 1969.)
38. *Life Against the Land—A Short History of the Pueblo Indians* by Mary L. Wood. (Timberline Books, 1974.)
39. *Bandelier National Monument* by Kittridge A. Wing. (National Park Service Historical Handbook, Series No. 23, 1955.)
40. *Turquoise and Spanish Mines in New Mexico* by Stuart A. Northrup. (University of New Mexico Press, 1975.)
41. *The Story of Mining in New Mexico* by Paige W. Christiansen. (New Mexico Bureau of Mines and Mineral Resources, 1974.)
42. *Union Army Operations in the Southwest—From the Official Records*, edited by the publishers. (Horn and Wallace Publishers, Albuquerque, 1961.)
43. *O.P. McMains and the Maxwell Land Grant* by Morris F. Taylor. (University of Arizona Press, Tucson, Ariz., 1979.)
44. *The Santa Fe Reporter*, June 10, 1987.
45. *Philmont, A History of New Mexico's Cimarron Country* by Lawrence R. Murphy. (University of New Mexico Press, 1973.)
46. *Ancient Ruins of the Southwest* by David Grant Noble. (Northland Press, Flagstaff, Ariz., 1981.)
47. *New Mexico—A New Guide to the Colorful State* by Chilton, Chil-

ton, Arango, Dudley, Neary, Stelzner. (University of New Mexico Press, 1984.)

48. "New Mexico: Between Frontier and Future." (*National Geographic*, Vol. 172, No. 5, Washington, D.C., Nov. 1987.)
49. "Santa Fe." (*Family Circle*, Oct. 20, 1987.)
50. "A Fragile Beauty" by John Nichols; *Impact*, Oct. 20, 1987. (Vol. 10, No. 53; *Albuquerque Journal*, Albuquerque, N.M.)

A bit of trivia about the author

A resident of Santa Fe since 1975, Michael McDonald currently works as an emergency-room nurse at St. Vincent Hospital.

McDonald, a Vietnam veteran and native of Missouri, travels New Mexico extensively and is an avid still and video photographer. He is active in the Santa Fe Trail Association, Mensa, the National Rifle Association, the National Muzzle Loaders Rifle Association and the Santa Fe Historical Society.

A self-proclaimed movie fanatic, McDonald's major interests include the Civil War, the Old West and New Mexico history. "I also do some writing here and there," he says, "and can tell you who played the Beaver."

A note of acknowledgement from the author

I acknowledge Marc Simmons, one of the foremost authorities on New Mexico history and prolific author on the subject, for the inspiration he has shown in writing about the state I love.

I also thank my co-workers at St. Vincent Hospital and my friends (especially Beth) and family for tolerating my constant New Mexico trivia questions during the course of researching this book.

A big thanks to Richard Sandoval, special projects publisher at *New Mexico Magazine*, for guiding a beginner through the publishing process and putting this whole thing together.